D0933766

Rollin' with Dre

The Unauthorized Account

Rollin' with Dre

An Insider's Tale of the Rise, Fall, and Rebirth of West Coast Hip Hop

BRUCE WILLIAMS

with Donnell Alexander

One World

Ballantine Books · New York

Published in the United States by One World Books,
an imprint of The Random House Publishing Group,
a division of Random House, Inc., New York.

ONE WORLD is a registered trademark and the
One World colophon is a trademark of Random House, Inc.

LIBRARY OF CONGRESS CATALOGING-IN-PUBLICATION DATA
Williams, Bruce.
Rollin' with Dre : the unauthorized account : an insider's tale
of the rise, fall, and rebirth of West Coast hip hop /
Bruce Williams, with Donnell Alexander.—1st ed.
p.   cm.
Funk family feud—Straight outta bunkie—The freak who rocked my world
—Black Hollywood—In tha lab with tha Doctor—California love—
From 4-H to death row—Un-Eazy lessons—The birth of beef—Darling Nikki—
Giving Suge his due—Beyond beef at Benihana—Vivian—G'd up enough—
More Money, more problems—Detox—The rebirth of West Coast hip
hop—Givin' props.
ISBN 978-0-345-49822-9 (hardcover)
1. Williams, Bruce.   2. Sound recording executives and producers—
California—Los Angeles—Biography.   3. Dr. Dre, 1965–   4. Rap musicians—
California—Los Angeles.   I. Alexander, Donnell.   II. Title.
ML429.W55R65   2008
782.421649092—dc22   2007041910

Printed in the United States of America on acid-free paper

www.oneworldbooks.net

2 4 6 8 9 7 5 3 1

First Edition

Book design by Jo Anne Metsch

I dedicate this book to:

My outstanding wife, Vivian.

My sons, Sir B. Williams, Mister Williams,

and Prince Bo Williams. My mother, Esther,

and my grandparents, Dock (R.I.P.), and Lucille Voorhies,

and Foressiah Collins.

"You are about to witness
the strength of street knowledge. . . ."

—Dr. Dre

" . . . and its weakness."

—Bruce Williams

Contents

Contents

Introduction

Funk Family Feud

"**Y**o, Bruce," said Suge Knight, with a flinch of that trademark tic in his neck. His raspy, Compton drawl was inimitable. "Let's go around here so I can talk to you, blood."

It was the middle of the decade of fallen MCs and we were standing outside the Westwood offices of Interscope Records, in broad daylight. My main nigga Andre Young, aka Dr. Dre, had just escaped the roaring grease fire that was his and Suge's Death Row label to build his own independent joint called Aftermath. Well, not entirely independent, but that's another story.

Together the Death Row family had sold more than thirty million albums in less than five years, unheard of numbers for an upstart outfit. Nothing like our run would ever again grace the music biz. The bottom line hardly registered it yet, but times were starting to get lean over at Suge's Wilshire Boulevard building—the Death Row headquarters—with those blood-red address numbers standing so high: Dre was gone. Tupac was dead. Snoop Dogg, Death Row's third and final meal ticket, had left to go into business with New Orleans rote record maker Master P. Not even Tha Dogg Pound, which was poised to be the next great hip-hop duo, was together. All around him, the empire that Suge had built so fast was showing more than cracks and fissures. The half-dozen lawsuits and criminal court cases he was involved in were fuckin' with his high. But the bodyguard-turned-mogul was early enough in the downslide that he was still very much feeling himself.

The Chronic, Doggystyle, Dogg Phood, All Eyez on Me. More shows and videos than I could keep track of. And all of it happened so fast, in maybe six years. Tumultuous doesn't tell the half of it. Shit got ugly.

Yet because of our history—history each of us made—Dre and I were bound to share space with Suge, this cat who kept it real through the most gangsta of tactics. In 1997, if Suge wasn't satisfied, niggas tended to get hurt. He had money and power and demanded satisfaction.

And at this moment, one of Planet Earth's top-ranked Bloods was trying to nudge me toward the most covert location he could scope out in crispy-clean Westside Los Angeles.

"Suge, no disrespect, but I'm no dummy, man."

Thing is, through my years of being *the man* next to Dr. Dre, Suge Knight had treated me with more respect than he gave most in our inner circle. But, now we were into something new, O.G. Hollywood rap beef: Uncut family feud. What was once the greatest black business since Motown was now in post-detonation mode. And somehow Suge couldn't hear that Death Row was over.

I'd left my car with the Interscope valet just moments before to run errands connected with Dre's initial post–Death Row offering, *Dr. Dre Presents . . . The Aftermath*. The circumstances had a nigga in Rockwell mode. I always felt like someone was watchin' me. But I wasn't *really* trippin': The front-row seats I'd been afforded to hard-core rap's signature moments hipped me to the bag of tricks lugged around by this wily, dangerous gangster. Even more than the sex and drugs and blingy-est of bling, I'd seen violence that would curl a lesser brotha's toes. Muthafuckas *will* go too far—if they're allowed to go as far as they want. That's anybody.

And at the end of the day, I sorta respected Suge. Without him there couldn't have been a Death Row. No doubt, there wouldn't have been an Aftermath, either.

"You wanna talk to me," I told Suge, "we talk right here. I'm not going around no corner where you got fifty niggas with baseball bats. I've been around the system too long, dog. I'm not dumb. And I'm not going down like that."

How in the *fuck* did I get here?

How did I, Bruce Williams from Palm Springs by way of rural Louisiana—former 4-H Club winner, former Jehovah's Witness, former army sergeant—get inside this crazy space? I couldn't say at the time. Prolly just chocked my situation up to the toll that hip hop just seems to take. As much hip hop can give it might take. Exactin' tolls like a motherfucker. In the record industry, at least, everyone get fucked.

Rollin' with Dre

The Unauthorized Account

Chapter One

Straight Outta Bunkie

I wasn't the first or five hundredth young cat to come out to L.A. looking for something my family couldn't ever give me and end up staring at a special brand of trouble.

Two towns east of Los Angeles, Palm Springs and Indio, are where I was raised. In these sleepy towns—one a rich folks' tourist haven and the other a two-percent black farm town—my mom, Esther Lee Roberts, and stepdad, HQ, brought up me and my two brothers and sister. Intermittently, I lived with my grandmother in a minute Louisiana town called Bunkie.

I'm the only one of my siblings who had a different father. No one in my family tried to make me feel like an oddball, but it was simply my birthright to always feel designated as a man apart.

In grade school, most kids my age were smaller than me. Workouts weren't necessary for me to be ripped with muscles. And unlike my mother's children with my stepdad, I was on my way to easily eclipsing the six-foot mark. I never felt like I belonged with my age group, so by elementary school I was hanging out with older people.

My mom was the kind of person who cared about every little thing. Say she was out standing in the yard and some stranger walked up and said he needed help. She'd be worried if she couldn't do something about his trouble at that very moment. She would just marinate in minute shit like that. She cared too much—about *other* people.

Herself? Well, that was something else altogether. She trapped herself in the world of caring about everybody, not having any fun. And when things didn't go her way, there would be a shitstorm.

Ma got real sick when I was about five years old. I went to live at my grandmother's house in Louisiana while my sister, my only sibling at that point, moved to an aunt's house in Las Vegas. At Grandma's house, all of her kids were grown and gone. My grandmother was tickled to death just having me around.

Mom stayed sick for about a year and a half. Later on I would learn that she had breast cancer. During an operation to remove a growth, surgeons contaminated my mother's body. She contracted hepatitis, turning a strange off-brown from her head to her toes. Get this: My mother never sued.

"At least the hospital didn't charge me," Mom reasoned.

That was my mother. She just sorta absorbed life's blows.

Tiny and rural as it was, my Louisiana town felt the most like home. My uncles were great, young adult role models—especially Dock—who really connected with me. Grandma, who doted on me and made me feel special, provided a loving environment, unlike the crib in Cali, which was constantly in turmoil. My mother and stepdad did not get along very well.

Eventually my mom got better enough that I could go back to California. The Louisiana life was fine, but every kid wants to be with his mother at the end of the day.

No sooner had I settled back into my Cali home than Grandma fell ill. Even *I* knew the prognosis before the diagnosis got voice: Grandma had gotten attached to me. It hurt her when I left, and she became sad and physically vulnerable. So I went back. And forth. And back and forth. One year in Palm Springs, California, and one in Bunkie, Louisiana. I developed a Bayou accent thick enough to attest to my comfort in the South. As much as I loved Louisiana and as much as I loved my mother, a lot of my decision to grow up in two places was about making other folks happy.

Now Bunkie was straight country, almost to the point where money wasn't a factor. Almost. As long as the football games and races kept on going, it didn't bother me that there were outhouses at Grandma's place.

Regardless of where on the map I happened to be, money didn't keep me from having anything I might have wanted. We just didn't want much. Mom raised us kids in the Jehovah's Witness faith. Material desire was deeply frowned upon by JWs, so there was never anything I wanted to have that I couldn't have. Things were just there for me. I just didn't want anything. I was more into hunting, fishing, and sports. If my parents bought me a single basketball or a football, that was more valuable than a whole box of toys.

Being a Jehovah's Witness wasn't ever something I felt passionate about. I went to worship at the Kingdom Hall because my mother went. Going door-to-door across Palm Springs with *Watchtower* and *Awake!* magazines was a part of life, like the dry desert heat. I grew up on the straight and narrow. Hunting in Utah with the tight-lipped HQ at the head of our pack. No drinkin'. No cussin'. Nothing untoward at all. Smoking anything was definitely out of the question, especially because I was so deep into athletics. But the sports had to be unofficial; the organized form ran counter to the rules of the religion. We had Bible studies all through the week in our home. Then there were multiple meetings down at the Kingdom Hall of Jehovah's Witnesses. And those sessions demanded that we study for them in the days leading up to the meetings. My "thing," athletics, was in conflict with a religion that—honestly?—I wasn't especially feeling.

This was a problem; athletic competition was my true love. Sports were my *thing*. I loved football. I loved basketball. In Bunkie, I played every day, all day long. But when I moved back to Palm Springs, and it was time to play after school, I couldn't because Mom was so against anything that might compete with the Jehovah's Witness life. In her mind, there were magazines to be placed and scriptures to be memorized. She just couldn't see the good in me chasin' some ball around. If I got home from school early and then had to return to campus for a practice, my mother would get highly upset. She wouldn't let me go. This made for a lot of arguments in my California home.

I somehow managed to finesse things so that I could join the Indio High School basketball team. One night I was on the court lining up for a free throw attempt when I looked over to the corner of the gymnasium and saw my mom. Whoa!

Nobody in my West Coast family had ever come to watch me play. I sensed nothing good was gonna come from this first-time occurrence. What cinched this feeling was the really pissed-off expression Mom wore across her face. I had an understanding with Coach Robinson though. He knew about my situation and that I was a JW. So when he spotted my mother he called a time-out.

"Go see your mom," he said.

I walked right over to her.

"Let's go," she said.

"You mean leave right now? Mom, we're in the middle of a *game.*"

"I don't care. Let's go. You're not playin' no ball." I started to explain that if I walked off the court right now my team would have to forfeit.

"If you don't come with me now," my mother said, "don't come home."

I walked away from my mother and asked Coach to put me back in. He did and we won and my mother wasn't among the gym's spectators. I didn't celebrate. Nope. I panicked. It dawned on me that my mother meant what she said and that I actually could not return to the place where I lived.

This felt a helluva lot bigger than our usual family conflicts. My mother was my mother, and I loved her, but I couldn't deal with the way she couldn't handle me succeeding at anything outside of religion. She was mad at the whole idea of personal gratification.

I called my Uncle Dock. I loved my uncle and wasn't really shy with him, but I muttered a little into that old-school receiver. "It ain't really workin' out at my mom's house here in Palm Springs."

Without a second thought, he agreed to send me a ticket to Bunkie.

During the whole back and forth from Palm Springs to Louisiana, my mindset was, *If everybody's happy, I'm cool.* I just wanted to please everybody.

At the same time, I used to sit back and wonder: Who are my real friends? Who's really down with me? In both Louisiana and Cali, from time to time I'd be sittin' and talkin' with folks swapping stories and someone would start something that was supposed to involve me and they'd be like, "Remember when . . . ?"

And I'd go, "Uh, actually I was in Cali when that happened."

And in Cali it would be vice versa: "I was in Louisiana when that happened!"

I didn't cuss or drink or smoke. Mostly, I just felt odd and square. Alone in a crowd on two different coasts.

I don't mean to badmouth all of my time with the JWs. The religion had so much studying built in, I couldn't help but become a solid reader. And going door-to-door with those magazines, it never occurred to me to be shy. But it was a different religious experience, outside of the JW stuff, however, that affected me most. The event that changed my life happened at Second Union Baptist Church with my grandmother. It was on a hill at the end of a long gravel road. Mostly southern ladies, the people in this Baptist church were just real soulful people. They loved to sing their bluesy interpretation of gospel.

My Uncle Dock was real smart. He had been a straight-A student. One day he stood up in front of the church and recited a poem entitled *The Creation,* about how God made the world. It blew me away how he read the piece and the power he held over the entire congregation, which was on the edge of its seats. The way he used his hands; he clapped to make thunder in emphasis. He took control of the whole church. Everybody was quiet. Nobody said *nothin'.* They just hung on every word he spoke. They felt everything he did and said.

Dock moved me so much that from that day on I *knew* I had to be involved with public speaking and decided to become an actor.

One night shooting the shit up late in some Bunkie ditch with some friends—and their empty 40-ouncers—I mused about the future I'd begun to feel around for, curiously, in my heart and in my brain. Something real cool was gonna happen for me, and it wasn't gonna be in this town or with my mom back *home* home.

"You know what, man," I announced one time my friends talked me into taking a drink. It surprised me that the beer bottle gave me courage. "I'm-a mess around, go to Los Angeles, and be in the movies."

The long pause that came after I said that is something I won't ever forget. And then, damn near in unison, they were all like:

"Man, if you don't shut the fuck up!"

Yeah. Even to me that sounded funny. These country boys were my closest peeps. Didn't wanna lose them, too. Next thing you know they'd be accusing me of being like most of the dudes who usually hung around drama class—a little fruity.

I laughed and let them blame it on the liquor. And I let the notion go, just a little bit.

Chapter Two

Military Stuntin'

I went to Louisiana State University for a while after I graduated from high school. College came easy to me. Still, it all seemed a little pointless. Then a friend who had been in the service started talking to me about how good the military could be for a brotha. I took a half-hour drive down the road to Alexandria and sat down with a recruiter.

I took the aptitude test and passed with flying colors. "Whatever branch of the military you want to join," the recruiter told me, "you're in."

He showed me videos in which motherfuckers was jumpin' and runnin' and shootin' guns and my dumb, silly ass thought just one thing:

That's the shit for me!

The Army promised me a spot in the Cohort Unit stationed at northern California's Fort Ord Base. First came basic training in Georgia's Fort Benning. I came in with my hair immaculate, and my jeans creased. Then a sergeant went digging through my bag, looking for whatever was making my hair all shiny. He found my bottle of hair grease and tossed it thirty feet.

"What the *hell* are you doing?" I yelled. I did a gang of push-ups and endured an explanation of what can and can't be said while in basic training. This is the shit they put you through to start preparing niggas for war, to make sure they won't crack.

The Fort Benning brass made me a platoon leader despite my mouth. Maybe my first impression was somewhat flawed, but you couldn't say the same thing about my presentation. My boots looked like glass, they were so shiny. My creases were so *tight*! And I'd tape pennies to a thin length of cardboard and set it inside the bottom of my pants leg so that my pants would drop over my boots just right. The creases down the side of my jacket were so sharp you couldn't tell me shit. All of this, with my energy and my demeanor, showed I came to win. I came with *fire*. In reality I didn't actually like cleanin' no damn toilets, so I wanted to show everybody that, at the end of the day, I could not be touched.

I was in charge of our crew and had to make sure our collective shit was tight. Overall, it was cool being boss of the grunts, but being in charge meant that I had to pick up the slack when others in the unit came up short. I had to check everything from top to bottom before any and all inspections. Guard duty rosters had to be straight. Shoes had to shine. Bunks had to be straight, etc. Every little detail had to be attended to. It was easy to get so occupied in this business that the "Lights Out" command might sneak right up on you.

Near the end of basic training I was scrambling to get the barracks to an accepted standard of clean—ready for inspection—and, to my eyes, the crew's shoes were not nearly shiny enough to satisfy the crack o' dawn inspection. Looming close was a bedtime deadline. I had a few hours before sunrise and most likely would have gotten the job done. Taking this sort of crap was a strength of mine. So, I was reluctant when this white grunt from Kansas walked into the light near my locker.

"I know you're up here making sure everything gets right, man," said the one I recognized as Private John West. We hadn't talked much. West had one of those midwestern accents that made me suspicious of his motives. Stereotypes came easy to me back then. "It's tough for you to get your own stuff done. Here, let me get your boots. I'm gonna shine 'em."

I looked at him in disbelief. To myself I said, "This white boy wants to shine *my* boots?" That was a trip to me. He picked up my boots and went to work. It was a small gesture, but it stuck with me. And we stuck together. Both 21, West and I were older than just about everybody in the platoon. The Kansas white boy became my best friend in the entire Cohort Unit, a cadre that was defined by close alliances.

West was my roommate. More than my roommate, he was my dog and having him around made military life a lot more livable. We went out a lot more than the average member of our unit as both of us were actually of legal drinking age and could hit the nightspots. That was huge, as shaking a leg is second only to sports in terms of stuff that really gets me excited. I'd been on dance floors since way before I was legal. Whether in Louisiana or in Cali, dancing was my escape.

This was the mid-1980s, when music wasn't yet completely formatted. The clubs in and around Monterey and Fort Ord played R&B and rap and even a little bit of rock. And West and I danced with every woman who was willing and able. That meant some white women got asked to dance. Not that it took a lot of goading. Most of them were absolutely into it. Sometimes *too* into it. The inevitable racial conflict popped up when a dude who ain't really have no claim on some girl would try to get all amped on me.

The first time my roommate punched a guy who called me nigger, it was great. Right up there with the boots episode. Second time? I got mad at him.

"Can *I* hit somebody? They did say that shit about me," I said. "Why don't you let me hit somethin'?"

Some of the black cats in our unit gave me shit for spending time with West. I didn't care, though; that was my dog. We kept in touch throughout our adult lives. I helped him be a good soldier; he showed me that folks who become like family can arrive in unfamiliar forms. Anyway, these small-thinking haters weren't my biggest concern. I had superiors to deal with.

In eighteen months my rank went from E-1 to E-5, which was an unheard of number of promotions for such a short amount of time. The progress didn't come easy. I had to go before a board of superiors before earning each promotion. Seated in front of me would be a sergeant-major, a first sergeant, my platoon sergeant, as well as platoon sergeants from three or four different battalions. I would walk up to the board, stand in front of its members, and maintain focus. The board members would crack jokes. The tested had to keep their faces fixed, lest they be downgraded. When one of the sergeants asked a question I would have to repeat it. I did, quickly and sharply.

"At ease," Platoon Sgt. Major Lee told me after my sergeant-major exam. I really didn't want to go at ease. It wasn't totally clear whether I was being tested or not.

"Williams," said 1st Sgt. Gill, finally, "put your hands down, at ease. Just stand up, son."

"Yes, sir," I said. My nerves had gotten to me just a little bit.

Major Lee paused for a long time—just like in the movies. I could hear my classmates' boots trampling down the hallway tile.

"You know what?" Major Lee said. "You're the first soldier ever to come before the board and ace his examination. All aspects, head to toe. Your demeanor, the way you answered your questions, your intelligence and focus."

I was blown away. But I owed my becoming an elite soldier to Sgt. Hightower, my platoon sergeant, and, mostly, Sgt. Hightower himself. Sgt. Hightower had been keeping watch over me for a long time. This man was in great shape, kept his focus tack-sharp, and, most important, cared a lot about his men. He wanted his men well-prepared if the country ever had to go to war, and he pushed me to be the best that I could be. Most of all he was a guy with real feeling, someone I could relate to.

"You're one of the top guys to ever come through here. You have passed everything we've thrown at you, and you've done it fast," Major Lee said. I saw a smile creep across his face and understood that I'd become this man's protégé. And to think, I hadn't even understood that I needed one.

But I hadn't joined the military to study. I'd come for explosions and shooting. And I'd get that. As squad leader I hopped beside the driver of my Humvee, which was armed with an 81mm mortar, an M-16 rifle, a 9mm gun, and lots of live ammo. The job dictated that I remain in a constant state of readiness; we had exercises every day with flying targets and objects that I couldn't see coming at us. But I had to be ready and willing to drop rain on the asses of any enemy.

On exercises down at the southern California desert town of Twenty-nine Palms, I got kicked out of maneuvers against an airborne division. Actually, it was my entire battalion, the 421st Infantry. The other side had parachuted onto the field, and my team had already dropped in. We helped them roll up their parachutes and got inside their camp. Once we did that, this war game was over in less than four hours when it was supposed to go on for four days. That airborne division thought they was the shit, but we broke their asses down.

My opponents in those war games, Sgt. Ripka, West, and everybody I dealt with while in the Cohort Unit would probably be surprised to hear it, but these people helped prepare me for the rap world. For instance, I had a drill sergeant who just didn't like me. He said my music was too loud and I knew it wasn't, which made me want to go at him. The urge to get in his face increased by the day. I approached my mentor, and Sgt. Hightower told me there was no way to make the problem go away quickly.

"That guy? They treated him fucked up when he came through the ranks. And he's just treating people the way he was treated. I don't agree with that part of Army life," Hightower said. "The only way we can change this—and it's not going to happen overnight—is for you to treat people decent when you think you can't handle what he's doing to you."

This stayed with me. When everybody else—amped up on get-highs and peer pressure—couldn't wait to go off on enemies, I wasn't so quick to reciprocate when I felt wronged. Don't get me wrong, I had my moments of goin' off on suckas. But ultimately I tended to re-flect on everything that happened, and not just from my point of view. I considered everyone's perspective in analyzing the day's goings-on. The army helped me understand wild situations, volatile personali-ties, and—most unpredictable of all—the business of music.

Chapter Three

The Freak Who Rocked My World

After being honorably discharged from the Army and returning to Indio, I was a little bit aimless. A low-level water company gig was the move for a little while. I sang lead in an electro-funk band that had a bit of Rockwell flavor to it. Some of the ladies dug it, but if you closed your eyes it was hard to like the group. We just weren't that good. But a woman with industry connections took me to Atlanta's How Can I Be Down? Conference— the ultimate music business confab during the early 1990s—and I met some industry people. What can I say? The lady thought I was cute and letting her take me around was a lot of what it took to get down.

Ultimately, I knew my voice was extremely limited. I did not quit my day job.

But I did start to work on my acting. Twice a week I'd carpool with Adina, a nurse I happened to know, the hundred miles east into Hollywood for acting classes. She was finer than a motherfucker. She was cool and introduced me to a lot of entertainers. It seemed to be a pattern of mine: I'd always seemed to fall into the hands of some bad bitch who helped launch me to the next level. I love women. One day I'd drive, the other she'd handle the duties. Even though I had a lot to learn, learning the craft of acting felt good, a lot better than my hopeless R&B singing. At least I couldn't see any ceiling on my potential— yet.

It was 1993 and around this time I met a girl named Robin at a Bally's gym in Hollywood. I worked out all the time and ate nothing but tuna fish to stay a cut 205 pounds. I was doing my last set of bicep curls when I noticed in the mirror that a tan, hella fine Egyptian-looking girl was lookin' at me.

In a tight one-piece bodysuit, the honey was light-skinned with curly hair and all sorts of body. More than anything physical though, there was a seductive aura about Robin.

Now, I'm not the kind of cat who hollers at every girl who looks at him, so I started to position myself around the gym so that she had to make an effort—a definite look—to see me again. She did, and that's when I chatted her up. We sat down for a minute at the café; she ordered a protein shake. Next thing you know, I'm at her crib, gettin' butt-naked. We didn't even bother to shower.

Robin looked like one of Prince's women. So, I wasn't too surprised to learn that she used to fuck with that dude. Even her place carried a Prince vibe, with white and yellow velvet everywhere from the curtains to the carpets. Just before the day turned to night, her roommate, Mia, came in. She was fine, just like Robin. Except that Mia wasn't your ordinary roommate.

It was right about then that I realized Robin had more bad bitches than even seriously ballin' Hollywood cats. She reminded me of an Egyptian queen trying to build a harem of both women *and* men.

Robin started taking me to the freaky girl bars.

"Don't have no ego when you come in here," she warned me before we entered the first one, Peanuts, on Santa Monica Boulevard.

And sure enough, even though I was a good-looking guy who was getting a bit of acting work in commercials, I went in there and got my ego bruised up good. First off, a cat couldn't get in unless he had a gang of bad bitches with him. Then they'd let you in, but tell you that you had to have a tie. And if you didn't have a tie, they'd provide one for you—and I mean it was a *fucked*-up tie. I'd never wear anything like it. Hell, *no* nigga would ever wear it. So right off the bat your ego's shot . . . and you gotta wear a fucked-up tie.

The most gorgeous girls I'd ever seen would be looking our way and I thought I could get 'em. So, Robin showed me how to let the game come to me and get with sophisticated hotties. Robin was feelin' me. I used to tell her, "I'm just a poor country boy, way too far from home." She liked that.

It was true, though. I wasn't just spittin' game.

Robin's place in the mid-Wilshire, just west of downtown L.A., is where I first ran into Andre Young. One night, Robin and I were watching a videotape of the movie *South Central* when he came through with Mia. I'd been a fan of N.W.A., loved all rap music from "Rapper's Delight" through Ice-T. *The Chronic* had just come out and Dre, who is famously from Compton, mumbled something about wanting to peep *South Central*. Instead of sitting down though, he and his stout 6′ 2″ frame guided Mia to her room at the back of the crib.

Turns out that after I'd fallen asleep on the couch, Robin went into Mia's room and got freaky with both her roomie and Dre, which I'd find out a few weeks later when Robin got Dre to let her decorate his crib. She asked if I'd come along to help her out for $300 a week. Of course I was with it.

Dre just started talking to me that day. I asked him if this was the same house that caught fire at the end of the N.W.A. days. I'd heard about it on the radio while traveling down the freeway in Palm Springs. I surprised him by asking about it. He caught me off guard by talking about it freely.

We talked houses a bit. Then he brought up this crazy threesome he'd had in the mid-Wilshire District. Some chick he'd barely known left her man on the couch and . . .

"That was *me* on the couch!" I told Dre.

"Naw, man," he said. I could tell he was a little nervous. "That nigga was short."

"I never got up off the couch!"

"Oh shit," Dre said, rewinding the night through his mind. He nearly sounded panicked. "I just put my foot in my mouth."

I could tell he felt really bad about it.

"It's all good," I said, sensing he needed reassurance. In time I'd learn that Dre needed more than his share of such support on issues not related to music.

"Dog," I addressed my new friend, "I'm just kickin' it."

And I was. That was me back in the day. I wasn't really attached to any of the girls I ran through. And it wasn't as though Dre was some kinda big deal who I was about to be punked by. At this point, I'd already met all kinds of famous people. Magic Johnson. Half the L.A. Raiders and Dallas Cowboys. Comedians and TV stars like Keenan Ivory Wayans and the cast of *In Living Color.* A representative of MCA Records introduced me to Babyface and L.A. Reid and Mariah Carey at How Can I Be Down? So I wasn't really trippin' from having crossed paths with a famous dude who happened to like the same kind of bad bitches as me, even if he did happen to be in the middle of making over hip-hop music. We just got along cool right off the bat—he was smart and hella funny and acted interested in the acting stress I was going through—so he asked me if I wanted to roll with him that afternoon.

Basically, we never stopped rollin'. Dre just picked up the salary Robin had been paying me and I drove him around, handled his schedule, and fielded his phone calls. Every day I'd wake up, work out, shower, jump in the ride, and whatever had to happen for Dre, I made happen.

Dre needed someone to help keep his shit from getting too hectic. In the couple of years since N.W.A. began fading out of the picture, Dre had been shot in Florida after squabbling with Luther Campbell's crew, and he roughed up female TV host Dee Barnes. (I'd find later that people made too much of that. If that incident was as bad as the media made it out to be, why was Dee's husband Ricky Harris still all up in Dre's videos, directing and doing other business with him?)

Within just a few weeks, he could give me a look, and I'd know exactly what to do. In Dre I'd found a friend, not some dude who was just a star, but a true friend.

Robin wanted to keep working for Dre so she supplied him with what we called the 30 Girls. The 30 Girls' function was to give all of us in the crew sexual pleasure. Each had a specialty. I see some of these women today with their husbands and think to myself, "Oh God, what has he married?" But then again, some of these women could look at my wife and wonder what she married as well.

One night Robin hooked it up so that seven of the "specialists" visited Dre and supplied him with a night of wide-ranging sexual debauchery. Afterward, my friend and boss was talkin' hella shit. "Man, I had seven bitches," I heard him tell some of the fellas. "They was all linin' up in a train. And Bruce didn't get none!"

It occurred to me that he didn't get the reason behind the ladies' visit. He thought they were friends of Robin who suddenly got the idea to get freaky with him, when they were essentially doing Dre as a favor to Robin, who, as I've said, had it goin' on like a pimp!

Dre is a guy who, like me, was taught to take care of the things that really mattered to him. We both came from unconventional families—his mother divorced while he was little and married William Griffin, the father of Warren G, Dre's little brother. Despite their faults, our parents showed us how to keep things nice. With Dre it was music. He fetishized albums like I took care to maintain relationships, and those thousands of albums he collected as a boy turned into a pure appreciation of music. My partner might fuck off just about every other thing not directly related to his world of creativity.

Spacey as he could be in those early days, Dre made one smart business decision that would make forgivable his countless bad ones to come: One day we jumped into my man's ride and he took me to his accountant.

There we completed paperwork that made me an employee only of

Andre Rommel Young. I didn't work for the label, Death Row, or for its distribution crony, Interscope. Regardless of the drama his music business would bring, it could only touch the way we worked with each other so much. As our time together grew, there wouldn't be one decision—not one brilliant artist he found, not one classic rap song he helped bring to life—I'd respect or be more thankful for than this. Doc Dre was the only person I'd answer to.

Dre would probably have lived the life of a regular nine-to-five dude had it not been for the encouragement of the adults in his household when he was young. A high school drafting teacher was pushing him toward an apprenticeship program at Northrup Aviation until it became clear that Dre's grades were too low. Instead, he moved into deejaying. His mother had allowed him to start spinning 45s at her house parties when he was just four. By 1982, when Dre was sixteen, his stepfather bought his first real mixer. Next thing you knew, he was rockin' turntables at Eve's After Dark, the seminal hip-hop spot on the corner of Avalon and El Segundo.

Emotionally intense—he'd lost two younger brothers before we met—Dre was always fast on the tech tip. It was Dre who pulled together the recorded sound of his first group, the electro-sounding World Class Wreckin' Cru. DJ Yella was the key scratch artist, but Dre, the younger turntable player, made their "Traffic Jam" mixes on KDAY and the breakthrough Cru single "Surgery" happen.

From long before I'd met him, Dre was known for having a bigger name than bank account. Dre had numerous children, going back to 1981, and the club DJing and Wreckin' Cru recorded work made him ghetto gold—street credible and famous but underpaid in comparison to the heft of his name.

A lot of people thought my man was well to do because he'd helped sell so many records, but the Cru stuff was made while he was broke enough to be begging lifts to recording sessions. Eazy-E, an older hustler he knew from around Compton, lured Dre away from his group through the promise of greater money. Then Eazy shorted Dre, too. Andre Young earned Eric Wright millions, but got paid in the low six figures.

For Dre, the N.W.A. period had been a surprisingly bitter learning experience. Yeah, Dre made an international name for himself because of his association with the group. On the other hand, though, he had watched his good friend Eazy—a guy he had made into a star by cobbling together the amateur rapper's rhymes line by line—short him while in alignment with talent manager Jerry Heller. When we met, it was obvious Dre was coming out of a difficult time. If it weren't for bodyguard-turned-businessman Marion "Suge" Knight, this cat might still be mired in a one-sided contract with Eazy's Ruthless Records. Andre Young might have been a genius in the studio, but in the real world, Dr. Dre needed people to carry the ball for him.

Chapter Four

Black Hollywood

It was 1994, and Dre was doing time in a Pasadena jailhouse for a drunk driving conviction when he had to get permission for a work release trip to make the video "Keep They Heads Ringin'," the first single from the soundtrack for the low-budget New Line comedy *Friday*. Former N.W.A. member Ice Cube, who starred in the film with Chris Tucker, wrote the thing with DJ Pooh. Coproduced it, too. The ties here were deeper even than N.W.A: Back in the day when Dre was too broke to have a ride to Eazy's production sessions, Pooh was one the few cats who would drive my man to the studio. F. Gary Gray, who directed the video for W.C. and the Madd Circle's seminal single "Dress Code," directed the film and was doing the video, which made the whole thing a family affair. Or at least that's what Dre said. What did my country ass know?

I scooped Dre up at that facility and drove him to the Burbank Airport, where we left the BMW. The shoot was set for an airplane hangar out around the Grapevine, a mountain-bound highway route about thirty miles north of Los Angeles. A helicopter would bring us in. I was up front with the pilot and Dre was in the back.

Man, when we dropped down next to that hangar, there were a couple of hundred people, all looking upward at us. They looked as if they were awaiting President Clinton or someone famous. The feeling in my heart was off the hook, impossible to describe. Even though this throng of people was watching Dre, I really felt a part of it.

"Dre!" I hollered to be heard above the crowd, "this is the shit, dog!"

I had no idea how much of a big deal all of this would be. The song would do serious work, in terms of transitioning Dre from his early work's gangsta rap ghetto. These other cats and I weren't that close yet. But I knew the film was going to be a comedy classic. Mainstream Hollywood was shocked at how the film performed; the suits couldn't see that weed and hip hop were going to be an enduring blend. *Friday* helped establish a new brand of film biz player. And the helicopter ride itself was a little like a metaphor for my career: I thought the army had given me a wild ride. Hollywood was about to take me to unimagined heights.

Three years earlier, "Deep Cover," the song from the film of the same name, had kicked off Death Row by introducing the world to Snoop Doggy Dogg. And eighteen months later, *The Chronic* was turning my boss and the label he co-owned into hip hop's main shit stains.

As Dre's status got higher and higher, I wanted his business to be more straight. Anything that could make it easier on him, I wanted to happen, tenfold. When you see a cat in entertainment doing it the way you want to do it, you do it extra well. You didn't want to be the person who fucked it off. I was the cat who got the numerous wild-card dudes in the crew actin' right. I'd make them stop wildin' out. I was the laid-back one, but the first one to stop the bullshit before it escalated. If I had to take someone outside and let him speak the piece nobody else around Death Row was tryin' to hear, I did that. And when it was necessary to scream on a nigga, that was my gig, too. In time I'd earn the nickname Captain Curseout.

When Dre stepped outside the studio, his world was heavy on grub, parties, fucking, and late-night highs. Sounds like the best gig ever, right? Thing is, I never really had fun, because I was always making sure everyone else was in line. Even in these freewheeling early days of Death Row, the energy could, out of nowhere, turn oppressively gangsta. And I had to be on point. It started wearing on me early. Where once I would go out dancing to counter the regimentation of military life, now I found I didn't want to dance at all anymore. There just didn't seem room for it as a top hard core rap lieutenant.

What's fucked up is that for more than five years my salary remained $300 a week—same as what I made assisting Robin. No insurance, no benefits. Dre's accountant signed my checks. As much of a whirlwind as his day-to-day reality was, there wasn't a real reason for the boss to know, short of me complaining. And, again, I saw my job as making certain the Doctor had less drama, not more.

Wait a minute. It's wrong to say that I *never* had fun. There was that one deep-sea fishing trip we took to Hawaii. It was me, Dre, the Dallas rapper known as The D.O.C., the upstart writer-producer Sam Sneed, and a few other cats. The mix brought out my inclination to show out. Some of the best moments of my life featured laughter on that boat floating off the coast of Maui. It's hard to complain about your work when it's got you chillin' in Hawaii with your boss beaming on a deck chair in the background holding a drink.

Dre's kind of quiet sometimes. More than anyone I've ever hung around, he feeds off other people's energy. And D.O.C. and Sam Sneed were just bright, amped, hilarious cats. The D.O.C. was a natural-born performer and could have been one of the greatest rappers ever, in my opinion. Dre said that Hawaii trip, with all that raw energy and humor floating around, was like the feel of his favorite recording session. All that was missing was a soundboard.

I savored that trip long after I returned to the mainland and was back to returning rental items and assuring studio managers that the entourage would leave their space on time and intact. Back in Hollywood I was like a hip-hop version of my mother, just working and caring about everybody else and never allowing myself to have much of a good time. That trip to me was the kind of unapologetic fun I just couldn't have growing up. Out on the boat we were competitive about who caught what fish, how many, and how big. But the feeling never stopped being light. Hawaii's not just gonna *stop* being Hawaii. The feeling of deep-sea fishing out there in all that beauty might have been gangsta Hollywood's first great gift to me.

We did a video for Snoop Dogg down at a house deep in the 'hood. Not "What's My Name?" the one in which I played a dog-catcher, but another from that first album, *Doggystyle*. And the producer, Ben Bassmore, managed to book us into a house right in the middle of Blood territory. Snoop, of course, is a Crip. Bassmore was from Detroit so he didn't have a clue.

When I arrived for the start of the shoot, a bunch of benign-looking Bloods were gathered on the corner of our street, and through the day you could feel their energy building and building. First the gang members started drinkin'. Then some music played, and they began to dance. Their looks were a little more cunning now. They weren't so friendly anymore. There was a grind on.

Wow, I thought, what's going down? It was my job to think out that sort of thing as early as possible. Although we didn't normally hire security, Death Row had called the Nation of Islam to visit the set, just in case.

Upon entering this tiny, narrow house, I saw Snoop in the living room, sitting in a chair. I stood right next to him. There was nothing behind us but a window and a wall. We only talked a little, because Snoop was at work. I looked up and all of those motherfuckin' Bloods from the corner were up in the crib!

Aw, shit. Of course I didn't have a gun, but no one had any protection. Where was security?

A Blood walked straight up to Snoop.

"What's up with that 'blood clot' in your song?"

He was referring to the line on "What's My Name?" where Snoop says "I kill dem blood clots." Among yardies in Jamaica, blood clot means something close to "motherfucker." These Bloods took the shit as a diss. But this ain't Kingston. We were some L.A. music biz niggas. I was next to Snoop, and the Bloods took up the bulk of space between us and the back of this house. Our people were mixed in between them.

"What's up with 'blood clot,' nigga?" dude asked once more. It felt like a standoff.

My eyes continued to scan the increasingly crowded room, quickly. Where the fuck was them Muslims?

"Mayn," Snoop said, "these just songs, you know?"

That kind of made the tensions release a little bit. Just then the Nation of Islam guards showed up.

"Let's go out the back," said the lead guy.

"Man, I ain't goin' out the motherfuckin' back. We goin' out the motherfuckin' front," Snoop told him.

The video star was cool, if somewhat distracted. I took the head of NOI security off to the side once things got back to normal.

"Where *were* you guys when all the shit was goin' down?" I asked. His answer wasn't even sufficient enough to remember. No answer would have been good enough for my standards.

The video turned out tight, though.

My work was hands-on, somebody's-gotta-do-it-action. Gigs that defied all job descriptions. And it wasn't the kind of shit anyone in their right mind would want to do.

For example, Shaquille O'Neal wanted to get some music done. So I got to have some conversations with Shaq, which was cool.

"Dre likes the way you rap," I told him. "He says that for a big man, you got flow. He wanna do somethin' for you."

But Shaq didn't understand that when you get the record companies involved there's gonna be way too much bullshit. One reason athletes can't make good records is that they're way too used to following the rules. Music happens on the fly, against the grain. Jocks don't get that.

And Shaq's album wasn't what it could have been. He really did have enough of a flow that even halfway bumpin' beats would have made a famous, charismatic nigga like him *TRL* material. Dre heard an early version of the Jive album and he loaded up some alternate beats for me to deliver to Shaq along with a message:

"I listened to the album," Dre said, "and I think he should redo it."

And he wanted me to go tell it to the mountain man.

Now, can you imagine me being at Shaq's crib? We're in his kitchen, listening on a tiny boombox—just to get a sound that's more realistic than an expensive sound system—and I'm in his face breaking the news to him that this thing he's put so much love and effort into just won't be cutting the mustard.

"Yo, you need to redo the album."

Big-ass, rich-ass Shaq had to be thinking, "Who is *this* mother-fucker?"

I knew Shaq for a little bit, so it wasn't like I was just coming out of nowhere. He heard me out, and I think he respected me more for it, cuz me and Shaq's conversations wouldn't be just basketball or just music. Whether we were talking about the way we brothas in enter-tainment should appreciate the opportunity or how to market an album, I always felt like he at least heard me.

And yet he *still* ended up putting out that underdeveloped album, basically because of record company constraints. The label had rules based on dates, and he went by them. (Shaq wants to be a cop when he retires from hoops, you know? He's *really* into the rules.) The sad thing is, dude can flow well for a big man. For any person, really. He could have had a dope hit from Dre. And instead Shaq has remained mislabeled as a joke MC, just because he insisted on going by his out-of-touch record label's rules.

All petty ambitions aside, back when *The Chronic* was out and the recording sessions for Snoop Doggy Dogg's debut were about to begin, it was easy to feel like we had the world by the nuts. We could go anywhere in town—anywhere in America, for that matter—and be regarded as conquering heroes. If we walked up to any club, they'd open the doors and the crowd would part like the Red Sea. It's only right; our L.A. hip-hop scene changed the whole music world.

But there's nothing like Hollywood. The flavor is why I came to Los Angeles. Seaside, the town next to Fort Ord, could have been where I landed. It could have been Palm Springs. Or, I think on really fucked-up days, I could have just gone back to Louisiana. I shake my head at what I would have missed out on.

Some think they're beginning to get the breadth of what hard-core West Coast hip hop's brought to the table when they see *banda* videos on Telemundo that resemble vintage Snoop Dogg MTV clips or hear rappers spittin' like political Too Shorts on the Gaza Strip. But it might be more helpful to go back in time, not across the map. Black Hollywood's been a beautiful thing from the days of blaxploitation, an especially dangerous and sexy scene. Everybody's in bed together, now more so than ever in our rap-driven era. I can remember the Rick James comeback show at the House of Blues, his first after getting out of jail. Paul Mooney and Chris Tucker introduced him, as a means of representing the past and the future rockin' hand in hand. Snoop was in that bitch. So was the great MC Medusa. While Black Hollywood barely got its fair share of deal making done, it compromised by having big fun. Not a lot of classy black films got made, but we brought a lot of fun to the table. The industry needed us in more ways than one.

You got to be a bitch-ass motherfucker not to be feeling our ride. The only thing better than the food was the women. There were ridiculous parties until the sun came up, and Division One head to celebrate daybreak. You could get it in a bedroom in the Hills or on some actress's deck in the red-hot Valley.

And me and the rest of Dr. Dre's team got in on that shit without kissing a whole bunch of ass. Private party or five-star restaurant? Didn't matter: Our black asses got instant access. We had amazing whips with consistently fine women ridin' with us. Especially when you consider that Dre had so many hits before *The Chronic* and still managed not to be paid. Everybody in his entourage reveled in the good times.

We should have held on to those feelings, because the period coming up was about to be a motherfucker. Hip hop giveth and it taketh away.

Chapter Five

In tha Lab with tha Doctor

The first time I went into the studio with Dre, *The Chronic* was still doing its thing on record store shelves, bubbling up to crossover status. We walked into Santa Monica's The Village recording facility to start work on *Doggystyle*, and what struck me right away was the absence of anyone else. Dr. Dre beat everybody into the studio, except the engineer. And on some days, even that dude wouldn't get there before Dre. Either way, a session started off quietly, with the Doctor moving stuff around, checking things out and, eventually, messin' with the music.

Other members of the crew then came through. Snoop. Tha Dogg Pound. Lady of Rage. Within a couple of hours it grew into a real cool atmosphere. The success of that first Death Row release let everybody know we were part of a special opportunity. As the night took hold we all gathered around the soundboard, laughing and partying a little harder with each addition to the room. Nate Dogg is in the house. Then there goes Dre's very first protégé, Mr. "Funky Enough" D.O.C. Some cats you've never heard of and never will. They all came in with no intention but to groove and, if they were lucky, get loose on the mic. Dre might start the music going with just an idea, a loose collection of sounds he had in his head.

Or he might start by fooling around on a drum machine. It was crazy, you'd see this guy start makin' the beginning of the structure of a beat, and when he hit on something good and the soundscape took shape, the MCs pulled out their pens and scrambled for flat surfaces to write on. Look around the room, all you saw was weed smokin' and drink cups. You saw heads bobbin' and noddin' and everybody writin'. Everybody who's a rapper was doing some type of writing.

Dre feeds off what the streets provide. That's vibe as well as subject. So who was around and how they got down counted for everything during those sessions. Every rapper was street. They oozed that curb-side ghetto feeling. George Clinton, a guest on those *Doggystyle* sessions, helped keep it funky, and not just with the music: His body odor was funky.

Death Row's maestro was different. Over the course of a session you might catch him in half a dozen different T-shirts. He sweats heavily while making his music, and every couple of hours he slipped off one damp tee, replacing it with another. He wanted to stay fresh just like he wanted the music to be crisp. And as the party got doper the producer would continue to work on the beat. Dre added things and messed nonstop with two hundred little elements of sound.

Sometimes he'd be in the middle of makin' somethin' and you'd be thrown off, lookin' at him like, "What the *hell* is that?" Walk out the room for thirty minutes, come back, and hear essentially the same beat, and you prolly be like, "Goddamn! What the hell is *that*?"

"See! I had to piece it together; you just didn't understand it yet." The boss grinned with the glee of a boy playing in the sandbox. And before you knew it, we had a new Death Row song. We might have four or five. It just depended on the vibe. Night to night the numbers and faces varied. Still, there was always a crowd of people. More chaos, more noise. Steady shit-talkin'. The fun motivated us and made us better. The artists got a quick response to their music. The reaction was immediate and real.

That's what the whole thing was about: Hennessy and Weed and Let's Make Some Dope-Ass Music!

When I first started comin' around Death Row, I didn't smoke. Shoot, cussin' wasn't even something I did until a couple of years before I met the Doctor. Anyway, Dre used to try to get me to hit the weed every once in a while. He didn't ask me to do this a lot, because—contrary to his image and what most people think—Dre doesn't smoke in his cars and mostly smokes only with bitches.

"Man, you smoke some of that weed *before* you hit the pussy," Dre would tell me, "it's gonna be some bomb-ass pussy."

And I'd be like, "Yeah, I'm-a try it one day. I'm-a try it. . . ." But I was always reluctant.

I'd been *around* weed before. I'd taken a puff on it here and there. But back then, whenever I tried it, there was seeds and shit in it. The weed would be poppin' and whatnot.

I was like, "Y'all can keep that shit!"

And then Snoop, who smoked all the time, used to tell me: "Man, the day you smoke, I'm gonna get you so motherfuckin' *hiiiigh*. . . ."

"Whatever man," I'd say and just laugh it off.

It went on this way for about four years, with everybody smokin' all around me. But the funny thing is that no matter how persistent Snoop was, I didn't smoke first with Snoop. I smoked with The D.O.C.

And I couldn't have chosen a wilder partner. Ya see, Tupac got tons of ink for wildin' out. And Suge raised the bar pretty high. But The D.O.C.—born in Dallas as Tracy Curry—took a backseat to no one in this category. A handful of niggas will take it upon themselves to let off shots in the middle of the street. One night parked outside Larry Parker's, a Beverly Hills hip-hop restaurant we used to frequent after the nightclubs closed, guy hanging out the window of a car shouted, "Yo, D.O.C.! What y'all niggas doin'?"

"We just hangin'," D.O.C. shouted after the guy pulled over. "What y'all doin'?"

"We just drivin' around with all these guns." And he showed us a huge stash of weapons. D.O.C. had been drinking and smoking pretty heavily, as was his habit at the time. He grabbed one of those pistols, looked at me, and gave me a stupid grin. Then D.O.C. stretched his legs out wide, held the gun straight up in the air, and let off three shots. *Pow! Pow! Pow!*

Everybody scattered. Some ran into Larry Parker's. Some disappeared down the block. The guys in the car sped off and out of sight. And D.O.C. just stood there laughing. How many cats you know that will empty his chambers when it's a *Beverly Hills* street? The D.O.C. was B.U.C.(-ass wild)!

A lot of people forget his legacy, but D.O.C. was the one who had the first Dr. Dre–produced hip-hop hit not affiliated with N.W.A. This cat's rugged vocal style and sharp lyrics ("No I am not illiterate/no not even a little bit") rocked the nation right on the tail end of Dre's second group's phenomenal run. D.O.C.'s first album, 1989's *No One Can Do It Better* is still considered a classic. Unfortunately, a few months after "Funky Enough" hit, The D.O.C. had a post-session car accident that crushed his vocal cords, limiting the Texan to writing lyrics for other rappers who recorded for Death Row. D.O.C. coped with it, sometimes better than others, but it was sad. Dude was just a natural-born star.

Ice-T ought to thank D.O.C. for the job that put him on the acting map. The late, great producer George Jackson had wanted my man D.O.C. to star in the role that Ice eventually took in *New Jack City.* This was right after the accident happened, so D.O.C. opted out, hoping his voice would recover with an extended rest. It didn't, and at this stage of the formerly great MC's time with Dre, he was smoking way more blunts than he was writing lyrics. He and I were mad cool— we used to hang out on all types of occasions. And for the umpteenth time, The D.O.C. asked me to join him in consuming some Mary Jane.

We were at one of Dre's Calabasas crib parties, hanging out in the kitchen. All over the house there were women and music and all kinds of atmosphere. We were chillin', just doin' what we do. I was sitting on the food prep island in the middle of a sprawling conversation.

Okay, I thought. This seems like a good time to take that plunge.

All at once tired and curious, I told him, "Yeah, I'm gonna smoke with ya, man."

"If we gon' smoke, you gotta smoke *with* me," he said with his now high, raggedy voice.

"What that mean, man, 'Smoke with me'?"

"Smoke *with* me. When I smoke, you smoke. We keep it movin'."

"Uh, alright," I said, "I'll smoke *wit'cha* mayn."

The chronic was a foreign thing to me, having come up in sports and the military and rural Louisiana. Weeds and stems in with a little bit of Mary Jane, that was *it* to me. Hydroponics was a word I didn't know. But whoever grew this kind sure did. And, man, this motherfucker was hittin' that shit nonstop, and I was like, super-*duper* high. I was on some other level; I don't know where I was. I do remember we was clownin', kickin' it by the pool table.

I started mockin' D.O.C., the way he talks. I was clownin', and everybody said that I should be in front of the camera, because I was such a good mimic.

"Maannn," Dre said, "if you can act the way you're doin' it right now, you gonna be the shit!"

He already had his eyes on the movies as his next move in town. He took a hit of his own and thought for a minute. He looked at his joint, then looked at me, considering my history.

"Or is it just the weed, nigga?"

It's funny, but as shit evolved, I began showing less of who I really was, of what I do. I was still a young cat, not even thirty. But those things I'd set out to do when I dreamed over 40 ounces of beer back in Bunkie would begin to seem as far away as ever.

Dre told me that rollin' with Death Row meant that I'd catch a case, one way or another. I didn't believe him, since I hadn't had any scrapes with the law in my life. Sure enough, though, I did end up standing before a judge.

It happened when I was picking up some friends or fam of some-fuckingbody who were in from out of town at Universal Studios. I had dropped them off at the valet's station and made arrangements to meet them at that very same spot at the end of the day. This was before everybody had cell phones. Anyway, wasn't nobody else really at the place since it was the middle of a weekday. No cars, no people. I waited for a while, but the folks just weren't showing up. So I parked my car next to the valet—obstructing nothing—just so I could get out and take a quick peek around this one big wall 20 yards away and see if my folks were there. This would take less than a minute.

"Excuse me, sir!" shouted one of the Mexican cats who parked cars for Universal. "Would you like me to valet your car?"

"No," I yelled back over my shoulder, not even turning back to look at him. "This ain't gon' take but a second."

"But you cannot park your car here."

"Man, fuck you. I said it won't be but a minute. I just want to look around this wall."

Well, I looked back and dude was getting into my ride! I guess he was gonna park it regardless of what I told him.

"What are you doing?" I said.

"I going move your car." The valet's English was suspect like a motherfucker.

So, I put my prospective pickups on the back burner and rushed this motherfucker.

"I said 'no,' mayn!"

And I pushed him. I probably didn't have to do that, but I did. Thing is, I was on swoll back then, pushing 250 pounds. (It was my first brush with dwelling in the lab, which was a recipe for obesity with crab and steaks at Monte's turning into a nightly ritual. The alcohol I was getting used to swilling didn't help much, either.) So when I pushed this li'l motherfucker, he went flying and his head hit the ground. Then about fifteen other little motherfuckers in valet suits came running out toward me.

"Whut?" I said to the surrounding miniature army. "Y'all wanna fight me? I'll whip all ya little motherfuckin' asses!"

And I would have, too. But they came to their senses and dispersed. I jumped into my car, took off, and went on about my life with the label and the real drama and the music. Someone else must have picked up the tourists. About two weeks later, I got a call from a police detective. Someone from the theme park had run my plates. He asked what happened. I told him. He told me the incident didn't sound like much and that I'd probably not hear from him again.

About two weeks later, they got me in court. There's no valet dudes there. The judge was like:

"You're a pretty big guy."

"What's that got to do with anything?" I asked His Honor. "Man, I ain't punched nobody. I pushed the dude away from my car. That's all I did. Where's the valet? Why ain't he here?"

My lawyer at the time (who's now in prison—but that's another story), told me to be quiet and sit down. The judge was mad because I asked questions. He hit me with a thousand-dollar fine, two years on probation, and forty hours of community service.

"Well, now you got a case now too, nigga!" Dre said between heavy gales of laughter, when we met up again. Everyone thought that shit was funny just because I was the well-behaved cat of the clique.

And I couldn't say a damn thing, except:

"Ain't this a bitch!"

I've been passed out drunk twice in my life. The last time, I looked up, saw Dr. Dre's face, and said, "Oh, no. Not you again!"

Dre, video producer Ben Bassmore, and myself had broken out for the Friday's in Marina Del Rey. I can't rightly say if the meal was breakfast, lunch, or dinner. Mostly we were about the drinks. Long Island Iced Teas, if you could call them that.

Dre made a face like his Long Island had been flavored with a faint, tan crayon. Drinking wasn't really my thing, but even I realized the drinks were lame.

"These are weak!" I told our waiter. "If I taste anything at all, it's juice. Double 'em up."

We drank the replacements and split, thinking this was no place to do serious drinking if we had to go through all that to get a Long Island right.

Next stop was over in Inglewood. The Townhouse was a little old spot where elderly people got drunk. In the spot's favor was the fact that its bartenders knew how to put together a proper Long Island Iced Tea.

Well before sundown, Dre and I were tore down to the ground, just hecka hammered. It had been one Long Island after another. When we walked out of The Townhouse, Ben threw up. He ended up sitting on the sidewalk.

Aw man, I thought, this motherfucker is *done*.

We dropped him off at his crib, then lit out north for Santa Monica and found a club set inside a mall. Fucked up as we were, the sight we beheld was almost enough to sober us up. Almost.

Bitches!

Wall to wall. There were fine, fine women up in there.

"Oooohhh!" I squealed out loud. It could be that I rubbed my hands together, too.

The nightclub was hot, and I don't mean it was dope. The temperature and humidity was high like a motherfucker. All I could think of was making it to the back patio where I'd at least have a chance to breathe. Of course, everyone wanted to talk to Dre, so we didn't make much progress beyond the front door. I felt bad enough to call it a night.

But there were bitches up in here. That was a circumstance capable of getting me through these troubled waters.

We were shoved up close to the bar. As had become the day's habit, I ordered two drinks.

Bruce, I told myself, you are fucking up.

Then I had a revelation: This was not about getting hammered; there were bitches up in here. Don't drink that thing.

"Gimme a water."

But then I felt hot. Real hot. It seemed like I would fall down at any moment.

"Dre!" I tugged at his sleeve. "Let's go outside."

"Aiight, aiight." Still, he kept talking. The next time I was a lot more emphatic.

"Dre, we gotta go outside!"

I don't know what he said to that. The next thing I remember is looking up and seeing Andre Young. As was often the case, he was surrounded by beautiful bitches. They were all looking down on me.

"Ain't this a bitch!" I said to no one in particular. I felt about *that* big.

"Dog, you alright?"

Now he asked. There was girls lookin' at me. Half the club was lookin' at me, concerned, but maybe snickerin' a li'l bit, too.

"You alright?" one fine thing with a fat fanny asked.

"Yeah." I climbed to my feet. "Just let me get outside for a minute." We sat at the patio table. And it was funny to me how Dre could make his way outside when he actually wanted that to happen.

"Man, you was like, 'Bam!'," Dre said, eyeing every hottie in the spot. "You gon' be alright though, huh?" He had brought a glass of water. And I'm a pretty tough guy, so I said that I could do this thing.

Three or four steps later, though, and it was over. I was puking, mostly water, onto the nightclub floor.

"Hey!" It was the bouncer. He grabbed me while I was still lurched forward. "Don't spit on our floor!" He tried to rush me out of the spot, steering me a few steps before I wrestled loose. I was cussin' and fussin' the whole time. Spit on his floor? What was this cat talking about?

At the door, Dre raised his eyebrow and gave me a nudge.

"You alright?" he asked, knowing good and goddamn well that I wasn't.

"Yeah, I'm good to go."

We stepped back into the spot, but I just couldn't make it. We had to at least hit a party in a different part of L.A. while I lay in the back-seat and caught a breather. Dre drove. He yelled for directions.

"East? West? Whassup, nigga?"

"North, muthafucka, north!"

I don't know how we got home that night. But, to tell the truth, I can't tell you how we got home on many nights. Once, while Dre was on house arrest and wearing a special ankle bracelet, we were trying to beat the deadline that would be regulated by the county's auto-mated monitoring system. We literally rode a flat tire down to the rim and broke the thing in half while racing down the Ventura Freeway and running over a raised road divider.

We didn't just travel in the fast lane. We sashayed across all five lanes at 100 miles per hour.

Ain't nothing like the hot wet streets of Los Angeles, especially when you're hittin' the scene in a cold black Mercedes-Benz. Ragtop. Low to the ground with the AMG kit. Fresh out the soundboard Dre beats pumpin'. Ain't nothin' like it. I recommend it for everyone.

The D.O.C., Dre, Sam Sneed, and myself were rollin' on the 405 Freeway, coming toward the Slauson exit and LAX. We were supposed to already have been at a party. As Slauson turned into the Marina Freeway, Sam mentioned another, possibly warmer party.

We needed to turn around. I did that, right dead in the street, twist-ing Dre's Benzo 180 degrees. Right after I did it:

Whhiiirrlllllooooo!

Blue lights.

And I ain't got no license. Too many tickets. D.O.C. ain't got no li-cense. Sneed ain't got no license. Dre ain't got no license.

Usually, I kept two or three licenses. See, the local DMV had that scam back then. If you knew the right worker, you'd do your paperwork and pay your money up front, walk in, and get your picture. Just scoop up your new license, then walk up out with that motherfucker.

We had a different life. Lots of speeding. We got stopped by the police a lot and didn't pay a lot of tickets so we had a lot of warrants. So I kept myself a few driving IDs. And when the cops pulled me over I'd be like, hunched over to the side, flipping through a small deck of "Bruce Williams" ID cards.

They'd come back from their car radios looking at their notes like, "I got two or three Bruce Williamses in here . . ."

Then I'd start to pointing at my driver's license copy.

"I don't know about them other motherfuckers, but I'm *that* Bruce Williams!"

No such luck this time—we were just starting to slip a little. I jumped out the car. The cop was a brotha. So I'm thinkin', *what can I tell this motherfucker?* . . .

"Man, you know you made an illegal U-turn?"

"Yeah, I know." I looked this cop in the eyes, but really tried to come off remorseful. My acting skills were getting rusty, but not horrible.

"Who you got in the car?"

"Uhh . . ." I might have something here. "Just my boss and some friends. You know how it goes."

"Yeah, I know. Let me get your license and registration."

"Ya know, I got that registration. It's in the glove compartment." Timing of this next line was gonna be key. "But that license is a different thang."

The policeman started writing on the form he'd only just opened.

"Look, man." I nodded toward the passenger side. "My boss don't know I ain't got no license. I could lose my job, man, if you give me a ticket right now."

He looked at me warily, like, okay. I could feel him checking me out. "Stay right here."

The cop walked over to the passenger side of the car. I climbed back into the car thinking we were just about out of there.

"Dr. Dre!" the nigga yelped, about like I expected. "Are you aware that your driver doesn't have a license?"

"What?!?" Dre turned to me looking completely disappointed that someone in his employment would do such a thing. The crazy-ass niggas in the back were barely keeping their laughter under control. "Oh, man what are we gonna do? Oh, if I had had any idea! . . ."

"Look," the cop interjected. "I'm-a let you guys go. But can I get an autographed picture?"

Let me field that one.

"We don't have any pape—"

"Just give us the address," The D.O.C. interjected from the backseat. "We'll send it to ya!"

I'm thinkin': As soon as this fan turns and walks away, the keys are going in the ignition.

"That sounds perfect," the cop said. He wrote some numbers and letters down, then tore that page out of his notebook. But"—and here is where the dude pointed his finger at me—"*he* can't drive."

You gotta remember that we are *the* shit at this time. Dre's shattering music sales records. We can hardly go a block without hearing Death Row music bangin' out of a car. It hardly mattered whether we were in Inglewood or Brentwood, the Valley or Long Beach. It felt like we owned the town. What *couldn't* we do, really? We may not have had licenses, but there's no denying our sense of license.

"Okay," the cop continued. "Who else here got licenses?"

Oh shit.

"Don't even *look* at me," said The D.O.C.

"Man, I ain't even from here," said Sneed, a native of Pittsburgh.

This brotha was steamin' a little bit by now. We could kinda tell he wanted to lock us up, even as he cocked his head to the side and looked off a ways. When someone stops being a fan, there's really nothing halfway about it.

"Send me that picture," five-oh said through clenched teeth, "and get your ass on that road. Take your ass straight home." The officer sounded almost flustered.

"Okay, sir."

"We goin' straight home."

"Thank you, officer."

And don't you know we went right on to that party in Santa Monica!

Chapter Six

California Love

He puts the music in a circle because time's got a curve in it. Dre's prank called gangsta rap wasn't quite a linear thing.

Every rap track after Dr. Dre came on the scene was like a cylinder of time: A cylinder that at first comes off like a cone, rotating to the beat. And the beat is powered by words, nonlinear slang flows that tell stories back to front and side to side. It gets hard to separate the engine from the fuel in this funky time machine. Cuz to this conductor, words aren't words. They're an add-on to the music: pure sonic power, more energy.

Since 1994, I watched him manipulate this power. Up close. I sat at the board, right next to him. Not exactly learning how to tweak the music, but learning how to put a song together. I learned what makes a song work and what doesn't make a song work. Dre layered his music, never settling for a track or a performance that was only close to what was merely *close* to what he had in mind. He needed dead-on perfection. In L.A. studios like The Village and Can-Am and Encore, it went down again and again, like making urban head movies out of ether.

He didn't jack for George Lucas for nothin' to start his second album. Dre's got the cinema in him.

The way you put a song together is really a miniature movie. You can hear every sound in my man's music. That's why his brand's so strong. Dre put it to me like this: *Every sound in my head is just rotating on an axis.* If *one* gear goes in the opposite direction, or anything else, the whole thing's not right. If there's a component in your song that's bothering you or annoying you, you are defeating the purpose of your song. You are bothering the listener, whether they recognize it or not. And when that happens, no one can hear your song. The only thing they can really hear is that one thing that's askew.

Dre will fix any and all lapses and lulls right here, with the beat. He's not saving it for the mix. Let me give you an example. Choose a song. Since Dre's so futuristic, let's skip ahead in time. Make it that one from 50 Cent that everybody knows, "In Da Club":

"Go. Go. Go. Go."

A song like that, the first collabo between two heavy hitters, when it comes through the monitors everyone knows it's a hit. There's a tingle in the air, and you feel privileged to be in the studio. Still, even an instant classic like "In Da Club" doesn't come straight out of the womb all perfect. It needs tweaking. That "Go" part is nothing if not tweaking.

You know the little element, about mid-range in its sonic depth of field. It ain't 50 who came up with that. It's not even certain that he knows why it's there. But his lyrics and delivery could only take that song so far. There needs to be music—or, rather, words as music; percussion, to be precise—to take things deeper in the cylinder.

The beat would be bouncin', and even though 50 would change up his vocals, there would still be repetitive parts. It slowed things down—almost made the song boring—while we waited for the hook to kick in. So, the producer adds a counter-rhythm, a slight *nin-nih-nin-nih* pattern to speed things up. Now it's good. It goes there.

You usually aren't very aware of that *nin-nih-nin-nih*—a little speed blip. You don't casually hear it; on a drive-by listen, you are not knowin'. But that blip retrieves the tempo. Check it: 50's vocals were slowing to a drawl, drawing in the listener. He's losin' though, because I as the listener am losin' the beat now; I'm getting a little bit bored. The song is feeling slower. How his vocal is coming across the track of Dre's music—it's not that he's *sayin'* it slow—the tone and the way that he's saying it slows the verse down *when you're listening to it.* It isn't per se mechanically and temporally slow, but the delivery brings the feeling down in the song. It's funk, and if a song lacks that, Dre's not fucking with it; 50 needs to say this part like that to make you feel the other parts of the song and what's comin' up. So the Doctor don't wanna lose you right there. The Doctor uses music slyly to underscore.

It's like when composers do film scores. Just a little bit of music—*duh-duh-da-DAH*—and it brings up the momentum of what that character's doin'. Same thing as the vocals on a verse. You add a little different music, different sounds. Maybe none of the sounds that you already got—and it adds a different flavor to the vocals and a little suspense.

Are the MCs even aware of what their flows are undergoing? Step inside the studio today and ask, say, a Busta Rhymes. He'll tell ya: "Man, Dre amazes me. He's got me *singin'* in the booth."

You'll hear the Doctor bark out odd orders. "Do this." One unexplained utterance and a knob tweak or two later, and it's "Do this." And not one of these rappers be knowin' *what* the fuck is goin' on. In the best of situations, the new, raw cats who don't understand the creative process, who don't understand visionary perfectionism—and who does, really?—just go with what is happening. They don't fight it. They show faith even though a track might actually sound fucked up at certain stages.

And to a person, when they hear it all put together, each one says the same thing: *Whoa!*

In these early days, we'd let young cats come in and just vibe, see how it's done. We'd tell 'em just to set back on the wall. Hustlin' L.A.

cats would come out sayin' they were the dopest rappers and how they'd slay the competition if only they could get a Dr. Dre beat.

"Alright, get in the booth, nigga! Let's put it down. Let's get it crackin'!"

Nine times out of ten that beat would just swallow their asses up and they couldn't do *shit*. And for the rest of the night these kids wouldn't say shit else about their rappin'.

Not until late at night, all sheepish and whatnot.

"You know man, I got it this time. Just let me get another chance."

"Man, come on," I said more times than I can remember. "Dog, don't waste your time right now. Go ahead and get your skills together, enjoy what's goin' on around you. Then do what you gotta do."

The attitude was real productive. Suge wasn't comin' around a whole bunch yet. The business part of the industry hadn't seeped in yet. It was just pure hip hop. Everybody was just havin' a good time and tryin' to make dope music. But over the years it would evolve to where we couldn't do that.

The first time I'd met Snoop, he was lyin' down on the sofa at Dre's house, sleepin'. *The Chronic* was still in full swing. Snoop was still a teenager, and all he wanted to do was smoke weed and rap. When he woke up that day, he turned to me with those ever-sleepy eyes and said, "Maaannnnn, what's up?"

Back then, Snoop was shy in front of the camera when it came to video, and he was just a laid-back cat. A kid, really. He'd try to go with the flow. He'd try to please muhfuckas as much as he could. Snoop just floated through the world. During N.W.A., Dre had Ice Cube. The D.O.C. had been set to be his next major MC before the accident took him out the picture. Dre always had his eye out for that big, style-complementing vocalist. And he found one in this lanky Crip from Long Beach.

Snoop had been in a local group called 213 with Nate Dogg and Dre's brother Warren G. Maybe folks in town have just always been used to him, but we would tend to forget how the world was falling in love with this dude, because to us, he was just an everyday cat, just like anybody else walkin' down the street. When reality shot in was when we stepped out of town, on tour. You'd see people fuckin' goin' nuts for Snoop. You'd see people runnin' behind you taking pictures, screaming Snoop's name. Shit, you'd have to run to your car just to escape the crowds.

The Chronic on which the then "Snoop Doggy Dogg" appeared was so successful, there was a lot of pressure on Snoop to put out a solo album. He was that *next* dude. And the truth is that his solo album, *Doggystyle,* never was completely finished—but there was so much pressure to get it out to capitalize on the success of *The Chronic* that Dre mixed the album and did all the little inserts be-tween songs in just forty-eight hours. It was to the point where the label people had a jet waiting for us at the airport so that we could de-liver the master and they could print the album.

The crazy shit was watching Snoop go from song to song, city to city, radio station to radio station on the promotional tour. MTV? Oh my god! Hella high Snoop on the biggest music station in the world? In the heart of Manhattan? It was crazy. And Snoop just swung his braids up in there like it was an everyday thing. He wasn't a problem cat. He loved rappin' and he loved just bein' out there on the stage. And he got to love and enjoy bein' out there with the fans.

He also loved talkin' that pimp shit. He used to look at me and say, "You know what, man? Some people are pimps who don't know they're pimps. But watch the way women react to them. Watch what people say around them. You got them tempted to do a lot of things they don't do. Pimpin' is for people that *wanna* pimp, though."

I told Snoop, "Man, you crazier than a motherfucker."

Still, what he said *is* real talk. A lot of people got pimpish ways. It's the will to pimp, though that separates the playas from the pretenders.

Snoop told me I was in Tha Dogg Pound. Even outsiders such as Busta Rhymes would come to call me Uncle Bruce. I was kinda like a cool authority figure. My shoulder was the one they cried on. My confidence was sought out.

I watched Snoop evolve, get money, have certain people become involved in his life. But he couldn't fully capitalize on his fame because of his label situation. Snoop was on Death Row and his manager was Sharitha, Suge's old lady. That's a conflict of interest. Where's the bargaining power between your people and the camp that pays you? There is none. Sharitha and Suge just took him on a ride, preventing him from getting his fair share. Even though he was one of the most recognizable cats on the globe, his bank account was not gonna blow away anyone who knows what real money looks like.

I looked at the cats running things like, *Why would you let this happen to him?* Maybe it was a Crip and Blood thing. Suge and Snoop were affiliated with opposing gangs. But at first Snoop didn't really care about it; he just wanted to rap, to do music. He just thought the people who handled the business were gonna handle it in the right manner. You pretty much have to be an uneducated teenager to be unaware that your manager can't be the wife of your record company owner. They're double-dipping at about every level. And worse.

To me, the unfairness was painfully obvious. Niggas *will* tell themselves lies, though. Fuck what you heard.

Snoop had a birthday during the period that he was trying to finish his album. Death Row bought him a car—a BMW 850 two-seater; Snoop's a Crip, so he had to have blue—from an Orange County dealership. Not too long after that, the police had Interscope surrounded. The car had been hot. That crooked shit was the fundamental problem with Death Row.

There was so much money around, why not just buy a new one, on the up and up?

Our ride was so wild at the time, though, that no one really took the time to say, hey, Snoop Dogg is really just a boy named Calvin

Broadus, only the hippest child star alive. And even he couldn't smoke enough to numb himself from all the pain.

One afternoon in South L.A., a bodyguard of Snoop's shot and killed a gangster named Philip Woldermariam. This was still early on the scene and was huge. That case brought nothing but heat to the Row. It was all people talked about, but we knew it was self-defense. We made and released the long-form Dr. Dre-directed video and soundtrack *Murder Was the Case* right when Snoop's story was at its most controversial. A whole bunch of people in the business and in the media didn't like that. This was just before Tupac Shakur's trial in New York opened, and people were really just starting to get fed up about the thug influence on hip hop and on popular culture overall. *Murder Was the Case* sho' nuff didn't make the haters feel better. They were turned off because we used the allegation to sell records. But fuck all that, the project really did do wonders. This was the first time we did a video for a song and turned it into a soundtrack. It was the first time *anyone* had tried that. For a long-form video to drive an album project was unheard of. Our company was still real young, so every bit of credit we got for innovation counted.

When the trial began downtown, Dre wasn't ever in the courtroom. *Doggystyle* was a huge hit, and people couldn't stop talking about what was happening at the courthouse. So word began to spread that Dre and Snoop weren't cool. Tha Dogg Pound showed up, but Dre didn't want to be on TV going to court, so he stayed clear. I can tell you for a fact that Snoop had no problem with that.

You gotta understand, these two have a special relationship. It's not like the videos, where Snoop and Dre were rollin' together all around Los Angeles, sippin' on gin and juice. My man had some clarity about his drinking. (He wasn't imbibing any less; it was just harder to get DUIs when you were tossing the keys to ol' Bruce.) Dre was starting to stay at home more at that time. Snoop rolled with his crew. Yet, whether they speak once a day or once a year these brothas will always be cool. They'll always have the same respect for each other. Snoop knows how dramatically his life changed when Warren G put on his song at a bachelor party and Dre heard it. And Dre knows his tracks don't ever sound better than when Snoop Dogg is rappin' on them. Dre never showed up at the courthouse, but Snoop sho' nuff showed up at Dre's crib in the evening, after. Unfortunately, Tupac and a bunch of jealous cats at the label who put in showy appearances downtown talked out the side of their mouths about how Dre wasn't supporting Snoop. This heated up the simmering idea among Suge and others that maybe Dre wasn't a Death Row kind of guy.

Snoop had only a couple of years earlier become old enough to stand trial as an adult. He beat the rap, though. Dre was as happy as any man not related to him. Nevertheless, their relationship at Death Row would not be the same.

Tupac had been a labelmate at the umbrella record label Interscope. In 1995, he had gone to jail on a sexual assault conviction, and his album *Me Against the World* came out while he was locked up. The album, while uneven, made him a huge star. Suge put up $1.4 million to bail him out and the next thing you knew he was rollin' with us.

The first thing he ended up doing for Death Row was "California Love." 'Pac recorded relentlessly, and he had a lot of songs for the album that would become *All Eyez on Me,* the first rap double album ever, but he didn't have that first single—the monster song that would make folks gravitate toward the CD. Well, Dre was working on a compilation called *Stowaways and Throwaways* that "California Love" was supposed to appear on. That album was a cool bunch of older songs he wrote and produced that didn't make *The Chronic* and a few new songs such as "California Love." That version had only Dre doing the two verses. After listening to Tupac's massive collection of freshly recorded stuff, Dre thought his song could instead make a hot single for the newest addition to the Death Row family.

Less than a month out of jail, 'Pac strode into Can-Am studios in broad daylight. Dre played "California Love" for him with his verses still on it.

"So, what do you think?" the producer asked as soon as his track stopped playing. He could be slow and methodical in presenting new material if the situation called for it. "You want me to play it again, so you can go write to it?"

"I'm ready to go right now," Tupac said. "Let's do it."

And the nigga went and walked into the booth and kicked his shit. Now, 'Pac always doubled his lyrics—overdubbed them so that his vocals weighed heavy on the track. For him to come right out of jail, listen to a track one time, not write anything down, go tear it up on the mic, and then *bust the exact same thing with the same cadence and inflection* was fucking unbelievable.

Dre turned in his seat at the console and looked at me in total wonder.

"That's some incredible shit," he whispered. Even as new to the studio as I was, it struck me as phenomenal. What I couldn't know at the time is that I'd not see or hear anything close to that performance again. He was capturing a moment in time: Tupac was fresh out of prison, livin' the life in Los Angeles after going through a poor semblance of American life in his formative years. He had the Bishop role from *Juice* in his back pocket. Now here he was in Hollywood, trying to cash some checks and make some art. In that order and right the *fuck* now. Here was the definition of live performance. (This is why "best performance" awards are absurd. You'll see vocalists win awards for turns that were pieced together by a producer, line by line; it's the producer who deserves recognition. This Tupac shit was almost athletic, a performance worthy of Jordan in his prime.)

Niggas don't realize: Tupac was *workin'*. He was smokin' and drinkin' and bustin'. Think about it, the nigga made wack beats into hits. Nowadays, your average rap star won't even think about putting out a single without some mind-blowing beat to go out and block for him. It was never about the beat, it was about his voice. It's a rhythm. The dude was a preacher to me, he told stories. He let you know how it really was in the world.

If only he had people around him who would just tell him every once in a while, "You need to just go chill out." Out in the world, that is. Inside the studio, he was off the hook like he had to be.

I don't have to tell you that the song turned out great. The video for "California Love" really set it off, though. Its concept of *Mad Max*-ish desert partying came from Jada Pinkett-Smith, who wanted to direct the video. Dre and I drove out to Jada's house in Agoura Hills. She had been giving us ideas and explaining the whole situation when, right before the shoot, Jada freaked and said she couldn't be a part of it.

Why?

Two words: Will Smith.

A Dr. Dre video? Uh-uh. I knew the deal. Will don't like gangsta rap, so there was no way in *hell* he was gonna let his old lady direct no video for no gangsta rappers. Plus, Jada and Tupac went way back and were mad cool. Will wasn't trying to see Jada holed up with this nigga, out in some middle-of-nowhere hotel.

So we ended up doing our own thing. We were all in the video—Dre, 'Pac, me, and just about the whole Death Row crew. We did it off the 15 Freeway, on the way to Las Vegas. Everybody had ridden out to the set, which had once been a lake and was now a dry bed. The effect was to make the backdrop appear like a planet absolutely lacking in moisture. It was dope. We easily fell into our roles as partiers. Niggas couldn't wait to get into those Thunderdome costumes.

For some reason I had to come back to the hotel and found Tupac standing in front of the hotel.

"Yo, 'Pac, what you doin' out here?"

"Man, I thought this was *my* video, dog. Everybody left me."

I was like, *what* in the fuck is going on?

"Dude, do you want me to take you?"

"Naw, man, I don't want you to take me. I want to make them moth-erfuckers realize they need to come get me."

That fucked me up. We were supposed to all be in this together. Nobody should have been leavin' this dude like that. We ended up doing another "California Love" video because 'Pac didn't really feel like that was his video.

It's funny, but as Dre was just really starting to relax, Tupac's wilding was reaching its apex. He was losing himself in the Death Row role. 'Pac wasn't as wild as people thought he was. He was as wild as the people around him.

Hip hop takes a toll. That could be its calling card, the toll it takes on the artists who make it, the companies that distribute it, and even the fans. It wears motherfuckers out. You can't make somethin' out of nothin' without *somehow* getting taxed.

Dre put on the first N.W.A. album, the album that started it all, that infamous intro: "You are about to witness the strength of street knowledge." Before there was "Fuck tha Police" there was that bold declaration. We all sure did witness the strength of street knowledge. Has any other art since Louis Armstrong's jazz and Chuck Berry's rock 'n' roll more seriously shocked the world?

The whole thing was like a monkey wrench to society: Niggas who couldn't sing or play instruments making the most popular music on Earth. The brokest motherfuckers becoming symbols of material wealth.

Imagine Dre sitting at the board. We're all in one room. The only time you're on the other side of the glass is when you're on the mic. But that comes later. We're all in or around the board and the hungry MCs are searching for flat surfaces and pulling out their pens while he's making the basic beat, not the whole beat that fans will hear on their car stereos, but enough meat on the bones of the beat for peo-ple to write. It was a trip to watch all these niggas go from totally crazy to being completely dedicated, getting their rhymes together. I was blown away by it. Having hung out with these cats just a little already, it was clear that they played hard. Now, with the beat swaying and so many heads bobbing and hands moving rhymes across thin wood sheets, I was blown by how much work these artists put in.

Again, it's the innocence that stands out in hindsight. I can remember young cats like Lil Half Dead, guys with obviously just enough talent to shine on perhaps a single song—not everybody who came through was a Tupac or Snoop. And those guys would be coached to leave their street shit—the bangin', the slangin'—behind, just to capitalize on the opportunity in front of them. Dre was introducing them to the world, and what they did with that opportunity was completely up to them. Maybe the niggas who were best served by these early days of Death Row weren't the ones who went on to the big-time pressures and fame of superstardom, but the ones who got enough from their shine to open a small business.

In my memory of the studio's greatest days, there's a ton of unforgettable moments, like the late, great Roger Troutman playing the vocoder talkbox on the other side of the glass, recording his "California Love" part with giant flourishes, as if his audience were 25,000 people at the Forum instead of a dozen high cats out in the San Fernando Valley. When I eventually began dropping in on other production sessions, it immediately hit me that I'd been spoiled by those early Death Row experiences. Never mind epic Roger Troutman, even the comparatively sedate process of The Doctor piecing together masterworks was a privilege to behold.

A visit to the studio with this cat was a trip to The Most Hip-Hop Place on Earth. Dr. Dre's thing has always been the studio. He was never incredible on video and he never did a world tour. It was impossible for him to lose the sheer joy of making music in the studio. It was a place away from the politics and the bureaucracy of the industry.

It was an all-out big party. The sad part is that it wouldn't remain that way for long with Death Row. The hits came so consistently at the start from *The Chronic* to *Doggystyle* to *All Eyez on Me* to *Dogg Phood* that it felt as though the hits would keep on comin' and that the label would become something like a new Motown.

I don't have to tell you that the vibe did not last anywhere near as long as it should have and Death Row didn't come close to being what Motown became.

It should have been Motown-times-five. But then someone went and put Suge Knight's picture in a magazine. After that, his whole posture changed.

Chapter Seven

From 4-H to Death Row

The Shit Tier is a row of cells at Angola State Penitentiary, the maximum-security prison where I got work years before I met Dre. One of those Louisiana girls I met in college had told me she was pregnant. I had to take care of that baby or my grandma would have just about died. But after I signed on for the prison gig that my uncle David helped me get quickly, the girl's mom took her to get rid of the baby. I kept the job.

Myself and other guards at this penitentiary, one of America's biggest and bloodiest, would walk along that row with our backs snug against the walls. These cells were called the Shit Tier because of their feces-throwing inmates. They would piss in cups, shit in cups, let it ferment and percolate, then throw it on your ass as you walked by. I saw guards beat inmates down, saw inmates beat down guards, too. Built in the 1830s with slave trade profits, Angola has actually improved through the decades. But it's still a work farm, part of America's fucked-up relationship with black people, and I hated it.

But back when I was still at Angola, the Shit Tier was some raw-dog penal system business. The inmates got to be out for only an hour a day. They'd walk down the hall, get their showers, and then get outside for the rest of their time.

We were beginning to use this new thing called a black box that you put around the inmates' hands, better in some ways than cuffs. Well, there was this one prison guard I didn't like a lot, this white cat who was into whuppin' nigga inmates' asses. One day I saw him put the black box on this one *evil*-ass inmate's hands wrong. He didn't tighten it properly—and I didn't say a damn thing.

"Man, if you were in the streets," I used to tell this racist motherfucker, "these niggas would be done whupped yo monkey ass." This cat would just be lookin' for a reason to beat a black man in cuffs. Nothin' but a coward.

I definitely tried to talk to him about treating people with respect, but he didn't want to listen. So, what I did this one time was let him misadjust that black box. It was a security rule that only one of the guards on the shift could go down to the tier at a time. The other guy had to stay up in the control room—didn't matter if a guard was getting his ass whupped or not—because if the other one went down there, other inmates could grab him, too, and take control of the whole tier. About the only thing a guard could do is press the alarm button and call for help.

So this one time the racist prison guard got halfway down to the tier. That evil-ass inmate came up out of the black box. And that nigga started whuppin' on that white boy's ass. I actually watched for a minute. *Then* I pushed the button. He wasn't beat up horribly, but he never beat down inmates again as far as I can remember.

No, I wasn't a gangsta at any time in my adult life, but I could dig where my Death Row people were coming from.

That Angola gig worked my nerves so that later on it would take a whole lot to get me the least bit excited. Among me were the hardest men in the country. Hopeless. You get in trouble there, and you're going away for a long time. The only thing a cat's got in jail is to save his dignity in some kind of way. A valuable lesson I learned at Angola was that if you give the extreme cat a little respect, he's gonna give respect back. And as best he can, that dude's gonna try to understand you. He's gonna understand what you're saying; and ultimately he's not going to give you as many problems. It's the same way on the street—or in the gangsta rap world, for that matter.

I came from an unlikely background to be wingman for the last volatile popular arts movement of the twentieth century. You're checking out a man who was completing 4-H agricultural projects in super-rural Bunkie when he wasn't leading a Jehovah's Witness life in Palm Springs. You're lookin' at a cat who served in the military and as a prison guard. You're lookin' at one of the last people a person would expect to click with gangsta niggas.

And yet, when the thugs needed to vent, I was the man they could vent to. They knew it wouldn't go nowhere. The masterminds knew the work would not get fucked up. I got the stars to their videos, co-ordinated the wildest parties. On the business end alone, I'd come to see shit capable of making Donald Trump's jaw drop.

At first, rollin' with Dre just felt like a crazy dream. I was rollin' with the most prolific producer in hip-hop history—hot records out, everybody ridin' his nuts—and at the same time trying to hustle up acting work. All of this with the mighty and hilarious D.O.C. usually riding in the back. Everything was fun, even at its most challenging.

The first and biggest lesson the game taught me was that this was business, not personal. In the music industry there was no loyalty, respect, or honesty. It was the Shit Tier on a whole different level. Niggas would shit all over you if you let them. Artists and big-shot music execs alike.

Dealing with Suge Knight and the other thugged-out gangstas was crazy. These cats would come to me and be telling me things that were going on—things that at first I wasn't really tryin' to hear—and I was taken aback. But I kept it cool. Something outrageous would just explode in the middle of a chilled-out night and while everybody else might be ready to go bananas, I'd be mentally taking it back to the

Shit Tier. And the drama didn't faze me much at all, because I knew that someone needed to keep shit correct.

For example, I was working with Dre for a month before I met Suge. Dre and Suge didn't hang out; it was usually business when we went out because Dre wasn't really all that tight with Suge on the personal tip. Dre needed the money and power that Suge could give him access to, but he didn't need to see how those things came into Suge's hands. The first time I met Suge, we all went out to the Roxbury, that fabled nightspot on the Sunset Strip.

Everybody who counted in Hollywood was there. All the dope females were in there. A lot of the times I had to get dudes out of the way. I could never understand that. So many lovely, interested women, and all these guys would surround *us*. I'd have to be like, "Dude, I could give a *fuck* about your record. Go away!" Anyway, a healthy chunk of the Death Row clique had rolled up and we'd gone into the side entrance. We get upstairs, and from out of nowhere this cat pulls a gun on Suge.

What the fuck is going on?

It was kinda crazy to me. What had I gotten myself into? We were the hottest music label in the world, with second place so far behind we couldn't even see 'em. Master P was still making shitty little singles. Beyond NYC, Puff wasn't even out from behind B.I.G.'s shadow yet. Jay-Z was still recording *Reasonable Doubt*. And here my team was, on some *Wild Wild West* shit. Armed encounters were a part of the new job when regular muhfuckas were still gettin' tutorials.

Was the dude really gonna use the gun? In the club with all these people? I made all these checks and observations in a matter of seconds—something I'd learned in the Cohort Unit and on the Shit Tier. I had to anticipate what was gonna happen before it actually happened. Then I reacted.

I went to grab the gun, and as I went for it the gun fell on the ground. I scooped it up immediately and passed it to Sam Sneed, and he passed it on to one of Suge's men.

Then the dude changed his tune.

"It was just a misunderstanding," he said to Suge.

What was absolutely going on that night, I never understood. If they kicked his ass or just tore him entirely out the frame, they did it later on. Suge used to be smart about shit like that. I was just the new cat in the crew and seeing a gun pointed at Suge—the first time I ever hung out with him!—was buck-ass wild. Later on that morning, I learned that the gun had cop-killer bullets in it, the kind that explode on impact so as to inflict maximum damage. Yeah, I quickly learned that Suge had a lot of enemies and was caught up in some real craziness.

Man, I thought to myself, this gangsta shit is really real. It's not just entertainment.

Later on I realized that my actions that night had a great impact on all of my future dealings with Suge. Apparently, the big man thought, "Okay, this dude is with Dre. I'm just meeting him, and yet he's standing up in a wild situation. Why was he there before any of my boys did anything?"

So right off the bat I got a reputation for being a stand-up dude—someone who has got his boys' backs. I soon got another reputation—one that looked like a lot of fun on paper, but in reality turned out to be a nightmare.

There was a birthday party for Dre at this rented mansion in the Hollywood Hills. This dude we called the Party Man used to come by and we'd tell him what we wanted for the get-down. And he'd put the whole party together. We'd have gambling. We'd be the house and give the party people X amount of money and then clean up when they dipped into their own wallets and gave it all back by losing at the games of chance. Upstairs there would be a VIP room with girls who'd suck dick. Girls in G-strings servin' drinks. It would just be an all-out dope-ass party.

So we get to the party around eleven. Dre's in the limo; I'm in a

Benz following him. But all the people we know are standing outside. They're supposed to be inside, but the doorman isn't letting any of them in. Once I sorted out that confusion—clearly this was a misunderstanding—we all went inside and the party was full of people nobody knew.

We get up to the VIP room and there ain't no girls there. Everybody hit Party Man up with the same question:

"What in the fuck is goin' on?"

"Aw, the girls comin'," Party Man said, trying to reassure me. "Everything's straight."

Suge gets there at a little after midnight. About ten minutes after Suge shows up, the cops show up.

"Party over!"

Five-oh says it's time to shut the place down. And we ain't even got started yet. What the fuck?

Suge screams, "Party Man, get yo ass over here!"

Party Man came over and we were all just standing there in the main room of this big-ass Hollywood crib. It's funny, 'cuz as gangsta as most cats in this crew was, Dre and the Death Row crew's stunned expressions showed me that some real shit was about to go down.

"There's people in here we don't even know! Ain't even in the A.M. and the po-po's already shuttin' this motherfucker down!?! Party Man, that is some bullshit, and where's my motherfuckin' party money! And where's the money we had for the gamblin'?"

On this crazy, violent night, I first learned that my future would feature Death Row execs and talent shouting, "Bruce! Bruce! Bruce!" Whatever the trouble, my name was the constant.

"Bruce, check the safe," Dre said. Keep in mind that I was still pretty new to the scene. It's one thing to drive talent to a video shoot, something else entirely to have the head of a powerful label reach out like this, in crisis mode.

I was like, Wow, they really *trust* me. I was feelin' this aspect of the situation and was good to go.

I quickly grabbed the safe.

Then a bunch of hoods on the Death Row payroll threw Party Man into the limo. We headed to a hotel on Sunset that's now called the Mondrian. I forget what it was called back then. I'm driving in front, looking back in my rearview mirror and the limo was just *rockin'* back and forth the whole way. I mean really rockin'. They were whuppin' Party Man's ass.

We get to the hotel lobby, and Party Man's just waiting with the rest of us, lookin' pathetic and all swelled up and trying to figure out what happened. Now, if it was me, I wouldn't have just stood there, waiting. I know that if we go up to the room there's just more ass-whuppin' waitin'. But maybe I'm just a different sorta cat. I'm not goin' upstairs. But this motherfucker don't do nothin'. He's just terrified.

I got my room key and was told to go count the money. Maybe it's a result of all the trouble he'd been in since entering the music biz, but at this point, Dre's gone; he got a new bitch and disappeared into a room. Lately he had been developing a knack for disappearing before the shitstorm got too heavy. He was smart. His game wasn't beatin' niggas up—he just wanted to make music and have fun. As soon as I walked into my room with that stack of bills in hand, there was no doubt that Party Man would come up way short.

And then my phone rings.

"Bruce!"

It was Suge. "Come on over to the other room."

I walked to the suite down the hall. Inside was Suge, Party Man, and a couple of Death Row thugs. As soon as he saw me, Party Man had this look on his face like, *Please, whatever you can do, help me.* And I'm lookin' back at him like, *Ain't a damn thing I can do for you, man. You just fucked with the wrong niggas.*

"Bruce, how much money in that thang?" Suge asked.

Man, I don't even wanna say it, but I have to: "We short."

"How much?" Suge asks.

"Forty Gs."

"What? Party Man! Where's my fuckin' money?"

And Suge just shot him a look like, *ooh, you motherfucker, I'm-a kick yo ass.* I didn't want any part of this. An awkward feeling came over as I prepared to interject.

"Suge, I'm about to go up to my room right now," I said.

"Hold up, hold up, Bruce. How many bitches did you see upstairs?"

Now, that was Suge just being theatrical. I know I didn't even have to answer that question because everyone knew that Party Man didn't have no bitches for us at the party. So I just shrugged my shoulders and walked out the door.

They took Party Man to the bathroom and fucked him up so bad he didn't even press charges.

And that's how I got to be in charge of the parties. I learned how to do it big for a lot lower cost, and that made me earn even more stripes.

As exciting as all of this might sound, it wasn't really all that. It was crazy responsibility, which turned me into a high-stakes bean counter. I had the keys to just about everything Dre owned, including a wild hangout penthouse apartment on Wilshire. Like, I had the keys to houses and studios and fielded requests to open shit. It was bigger than keys, though. Suge, Dre, Snoop, the old white guy who operated the studio. Everybody had the number to my mobile phone and they didn't hesitate to use it.

I would get late-night calls to answer everything imaginable.

Later, when Dre left Death Row for Aftermath, we started hiring people to do certain things, and then I had my hands in a lot fewer pots. But in the beginning, when we were at Death Row, I had to do it all. And because of that, sometimes Suge assumed that because I'd do shit for him, that we were allies. He was mistaken. I might check a safe every now and again, but ultimately I got paid by Dre, and he's the only one I took orders from.

At the same time, it was hard to let my own ambitions go. I never forgot that I'd come to Hollywood to make a name for myself. My job was minding Dre, but I was still that ambitious cat. My nightlife had sidelights. And I wanted to work in Hollywood. As much as I helped Dre, it just seemed he could have helped me out more.

One day I asked Dre, "Yo, man, you gonna talk to John Singleton about getting me an audition?" Now I didn't say *tell* him to give me a part. I was just looking for an audition, so I could prove myself.

He said, "Oh, I got you, Bruce." But of course he never did it.

But I'm the type of cat who's not just gonna sit and keep waiting, man. So, I kept pushin' and kept pushin', and I got to John myself. And he was like, "Man, I got somethin' for ya. Don't worry, I'm gonna give you some speaking stuff."

And he did. I appeared with Busta Rhymes, Ice Cube, Omar Epps in the movie *Higher Learning*. We shot that at UCLA over about two months. Then I got another small role, in F. Gary Gray's *Set It Off.* I was feeling good because my acting career was finally starting to gain some traction.

At the same time, I finally figured out that everyone around me was full of shit.

Michel'le, the R&B singer who was Dre's girlfriend at the time and mother of his son Marcel—I was very close to her—pulled me aside and said, "You know, Bruce, you're breakin' Dre's heart with this act-ing stuff."

These were just small roles; they didn't mean much. It freaked my man out, though. He wanted me to be in total control of his personal business, not doing my own thing. I was confused; if anyone in L.A. knew what brought me here, it was Andre Young.

At my most frustrated, I only had to look back at the key relation-ships in Dre's work life. He'd gotten fucked over by the Wreckin' Cru after helping turn that DJ crew into an important recording group. His experience with Eazy was legendarily exploitive. And he was in a burgeoning tug of war between Suge and Jimmy Iovine. His insecurity made sense after I thought long and hard about it. In Dre's world, everyone around him was full of shit. I wasn't, so he leaned on me. I was doing so much to make the man comfortable that it really was hard to let my dreams go. But I did that—gave up dancing, then acting—because I could take it and because I knew I was a part of something historic.

The unofficial Death Row studio was out at Can-Am. In one of those early days, I got a call from there.

Some cat says, "Suge's having a meeting and he wants you to come."

I'm thinkin': Wait. I don't take no goddamn meetings with Death Row!

"Let me check with Dre," I said, before I placed my hand over the receiver. "Hey, D.R.! You know anything about some meeting Suge wanted?"

"Shit," Dre said. "I don't know nothin' about it."

"Well, should I go?"

"I dunno. Go check it out; see what's up."

So I go to Can-Am. That studio's no different from most, except that Can-Am is way out in the Valley and the lobby walls are loaded down with platinum plaques from West Coast hip-hop classics. It's a comfortable enough place to hang out—for a little while. Suge would show up five hours late. He had motherfuckers just sittin' around there. And I'm not that nigga. I'm not fixing to wait around for somebody for five hours, man. I took off after the first one.

At six o'clock that night, my phone rings.

"Yeah, what up? This is Bruce."

"Yeah, Suge wanna talk to ya."

And, to remind you, I don't really even know what's goin' on. I don't work for Suge. But Suge has everybody who works for Death Row in his office. They're all sitting on the floor, all the way around the office, after waiting for him for five hours.

Suge gets on the phone. "Bruce! Where the hell you at?"

"Man, I'm at the crib, gettin' ready to go to a video shoot."

"Don't you know we havin' a meeting?"

"Look, man, yeah, I *came* to that meeting. That was five hours ago. Wasn't nobody there. I got stuff to do, for Dre."

"You got stuff to do for Dre? That's okay, but you need to start doin' what I tell you to do!"

"What are you talkin' about, man? I came over there. Wasn't nobody there. I came over there, I sat down, and I waited. Then I had stuff to do."

"And what's this stuff about people callin' you and you never callin' them back?"

"Now who told you that?" I could tell Suge was trying to get into it with me.

"Roy and them said they be callin' you all the time and that you never call back."

Suge was talking about Roy, Suge's executive assistant.

"Man, Roy and them is some fuckin' punks. They be trying to blame stuff on somebody else 'cuz they ain't got the nuts to tell you they own goddamn selves. I don't give a fuck about Roy. Roy's lyin'.

"That's what's wrong around here!" I continued to rant at Suge. "Everybody's blamin' shit on everybody else and ain't nobody wanna take responsibility!"

I told him I had to go.

"Where the hell you goin'?" he shouted.

"I told you, man, I'm goin' to the video shoot."

"You ain't runnin' nothin' around here!"

"I ain't tryin' to run nothin'. What are you talkin' about?"

"You want me to come over there and get you?"

"Man, I don't care about all that. You can come do what you gotta do. I ain't tryin' to go through all that mess. You got people in there lyin', and I ain't got time for all that shit."

Suge was getting pissed! I know this because Larry—the product manager of Death Row—called me after I got to the shoot.

"Bruce, are you crazy?" Larry asked. "Did you know that you were on speakerphone?"

I didn't know that, not as if it would have mattered. Regardless, Suge never mentioned that exchange. Naturally I was concerned that the face of Death Row Records didn't have good feelings about me because I took a stand. At the video shoot's catering spread, Dre told me otherwise.

"Naw, man," he said, poised to pop a piece of chicken into his mouth. "Suge likes you. He says you're the only one who's got nuts."

As years went by, Dre promised to help me with all sorts of stuff in the entertainment game. I would develop an idea, but nothing ever came of anything. Great projects, but before I would follow through, something would come up.

"Hold up, Bruce. We gotta go do somethin' else."

Every day our crew watered a young tree with beautiful, strong roots. Lots of talented people, including non-rappers, were around us. And I would tell my friend, You couldn't *give* me the amount of money that you could *help* me make.

But with each new deal—beyond Death Row and deep into the next, uncharted territory—I'd hear, "I'm-a take care of ya." Years passed and not a thing materialized.

Chapter Eight

Un-Eazy Lessons

How wild is it that the people who finally helped me define family were the pioneers of West Coast gangsta rap? Even when you weren't trying to learn, lessons were being dished out. Just like blood fam.

In the spring of 1995, one of those lessons got learned at the hospital bedside of Eric "Eazy-E" Wright. Along with Ice Cube, MC Ren, and DJ Yella, Dre and Eazy had been the heart of N.W.A. This group made some of the most important music of the twentieth century. Dre's music took funk to a place previously unimagined. Before N.W.A. and rap music, George Clinton and James Brown had politicized funk, but never had the two forces been given such a powerful, popular marriage. N.W.A. went platinum without any airplay *and* drove the F.B.I. to harass the group via threatening mail. None of what I was seeing so up close and personal could have happened without the pioneering ways of N.W.A.

Years prior to making *Straight Outta Compton*, the group's debut album, Dre produced Eazy, a novice rapper with a pocketful of dirty money, and made his way beyond the ghetto celebrity the World Class Wreckin' Cru had brought. He had leaped directly from producing the sonically showy Wreckin' Cru ballad "Turn Out the Lights" to working on Eazy's solo LP debut. He'd held the drug dealer's hand through the recording of "Boyz-N-The-Hood," a single that took Run-DMC's hardness to a whole different level. Ice Cube, a nineteen-year-old

from Compton who'd written the song prior to leaving for architec-
ture school in Arizona, came back to Los Angeles and started writing
the album. MC Ren and DJ Yella signed on for support and, just like
that, a supergroup was born.

Big as it seemed at the time, the fame my friend found in N.W.A. was
something like training wheels for the ride that was to follow. Haters
took issue with every aspect of N.W.A., from its lyrics to its straightfor-
ward rhyme style to the Jheri curls that members of the group wore.
Dre's music had a rebellious quality to it that always seemed to mar-
shal together opposing forces.

Nobody complained about Dre's production, though. It was stark
and huge and serious, all at the same time, and the acclaim his work
received was so much bigger than the "Traffic Jam" mixes and swap
meet sales that his Wreckin' Cru work had generated. With N.W.A. he
became a music icon, the future of the funk. Even more than that,
N.W.A. prepared Andre Young for what real money and all the perks of
multiplatinum fame looked like. When Ice Cube quit the group, he
claimed to have made less than thirty grand for his work. Well, Dre did
a little better than that, producing as he did more than a dozen albums and EPs for Ruthless Records, which housed N.W.A. Doc Dre
did, after all, end up with that house that burned down just before I
met him.

But the way Dre got away from Ruthless Records, the label Eazy
owned with Jerry Heller, involved Suge, a baseball bat, and a pen that
the diminutive rapper was forced to use on a contract. Even though
they'd known each other way before there was big money in rap, Dr.
Dre and Eazy-E hadn't been on good terms in years. The first Death
Row songs and videos made Dre's partner in N.W.A. the focal point of
clowning.

Back when we first met, Dre had told me he really lacked the energy for beefin' with his old homey. He just wondered what Heller
had on Eazy that made him not separate from the old guy. If he was
robbin' N.W.A. and Dre, then you know he was robbin' Eazy. Maybe

Eazy was just afraid to stand on his own. Regardless, their beef, how-ever public, had only gone so deep. The two Compton homeys weren't working together anymore, but just because you don't work with a person doesn't mean you hate them. That the two were still ac-tively feuding is a misconception that Dre himself played a big role in perpetuating.

Then word hit the streets that Eazy had contracted AIDS. Not just HIV, but late-stage AIDS that revealed itself only as he slipped into a coma. Eazy's prognosis went from nonexistent to fatal in a matter of days. Nobody saw it coming. Dre had been in the Pasadena jailhouse on a parole violation when the news broke, and when I picked him up he asked me to take him directly to Cedar Sinai Medical Center. The depth of Dre's concern for his homey was all over his face. And why shouldn't it have been? He cared a lot for Eazy. They'd risen to the top together and transformed the entire rap game. All most people knew was the beef that was largely blown up to sell records. They didn't know that these two had been on the phone a lot recently, talking of patching things up. Fans gathered outside the hospital seemed sur-prised to see Dr. Dre headed for the elevator to Eazy-E's floor. But they were brothers, way closer than what could be portrayed in the media.

I remember the sound and sight of Wright's fam and business inter-ests fighting over his dough. Lawyer talk in the hallway as a man is fixin' to pass. That alone probably chilled Dre's shit. It fucked with me, so you know it fucked with him.

"Let's go up in there," Dre said, disgust on his face for the hallway shenanigans.

"Naw, man," I responded, "You the one who know him like that."

Dre walked into the private room, even though I could tell it was the last thing he wanted to do. The man had already lost two blood brothers, Tyree and Bubby, in years past. Now his brother in the rap game was knockin' on heaven's door.

While I held up the wall and Eazy's people kept up their bickering,

Dre talked to his homey, but it wasn't even clear to him that li'l-ass Eric Wright, looking childlike beneath his hospital sheets, could even understand him.

Who ever heard of AIDS taking someone so fast? If there had been time, I'm sure Dre could have said more, but he spoke from his heart and what Dre said was deep. If Eric Wright could at all hear what his good friend said, he would have been glad the dude made the effort. Eazy seemed as though he were sleeping. A machine did his breathing. Without the technology that made his chest move up and down, he'd have been dead.

"It's a shame that this man is dying and all these people are fighting over his fortune," Dre said. We went into a silent mode, the hurt was so hard. You say you're gonna reconcile with a close friend and then that person dies before you can make the decision real? That's some crazy shit.

Headed down the elevator, Dre looked stricken. And I wasn't doin' too good my damn self. We walked to the Benz. Dre talked a bit about the great times he and Eric shared and what he'd lose when this guy left and I just sat back and listened. Not a lot of people in town knew like he knew about the toll hip hop takes on everybody.

Chapter Nine

The Birth of Beef

The second annual Source Awards, held in August 1995, was the greatest awards show I've ever attended, bar none. Grammys, Emmys, *Soul Train*. All of them are pretty fucking boring. You sit there waiting for awards to be presented, for performers to come out, for commercials. *The Source* Awards atmosphere was straight street-chaotic. The first one, which wasn't actually televised, is remembered mostly because Tupac, who went to prison later that year for sexual abuse, ran up on stage during A Tribe Called Quest's set and disrupted their performance. That pretty much set the tone.

We were sitting in the middle of the front row of the Paramount Theater at Madison Square Garden in the Death Row section. The whole Death Row family had the first four rows blocked off. There were other cliques there. You had Queensbridge on one side, Wu Tang Clan on the other. You had the Bronx niggas. Everybody had their own section. Every intermission you'd start hearing this shouting:

"Fuck Queensbridge!"

"Fuck the Bronx!"

"Fuck Death Row!"

Nothing but tension. You could feel it in the air, like *somebody's gettin' their ass whupped tonight*!

Death Row artists came out and smashed the show at its start. The organizers had wanted us to end the show, but we were like, "Fuck you. Don't nobody give a fuck about the end of a show." These shows are so long that the motherfuckers performing at the end don't get a response. We were gonna open this bitch. Get in and get out.

Snoop and Dre performed. Every performer was in a cellblock, a row of staged bars and walls set under spotlights. They'd open a door and an artist would step forward and rap. *Cha-chink!* Dre came out. *Cha-chink!* Snoop came out.

This was the ultimate industry party. Everybody knew that 'Pac was comin' with us to Death Row—from the Interscope umbrella—when he got out. So we had a red and blue flag—representing gangsta unity—in his cell, with his silhouette. The symbol established 'Pac's presence. Snoop, among others, wasn't satisfied with the New York audience response. In hindsight, our crew was insatiable. (That's part of what made it legendary.) There was nothing Madison Square Garden could do.

When Snoop won his Artist of the Year award, he—hair all afro'd out—lit into the audience as if it had been sitting on its hands.

"The East Coast ain't got no love for Dr. Dre and Snoop Dogg and Death Row?"

He said it again, and the audience began to give it up. They had to recognize the realness, even if most of them cats felt like our success was taking food off their families' dinner tables.

I remember that the performances were all off the hook. The audience went crazy after every nigga not from the West Coast rocked the mic. Outkast won Best New Artist and Notorious B.I.G. won four awards. It definitely wasn't a West Coast night, regardless of what our chart-topping success said. The tension rose unrelentingly.

And when Death Row won for the *Above the Rim* soundtrack, that's when Suge spoke his infamous words.

"To all you artists out there, who don't wanna be on a record label where the executive producers . . . all up in the videos, all on the records, dancin' . . . then come to Death Row!"

And niggas went absolutely bananas. There was no doubt who he was speaking about. Sean "Puffy" Combs, CEO of Bad Boy Entertainment, had just put out Notorious B.I.G.'s *Ready to Die,* an album that Suge and a lot of people inside our camp thought jacked *The Chronic* hard-core pop recipe. We wanted due recognition. Biggie was a dope artist, but if a respected album is patterned after your shit you want respect. What's more, Tupac was beefin' with Biggie, thinking dude had been responsible for his being shot in 1993. Suge wanted to show the world that 'Pac's fight was Death Row's fight. He wanted to set the stage.

Then Puffy came out and said he wasn't gonna be beefin' and all that. Dre looked at me and I looked at him as the crowd was getting more and more amped.

"How in the *fuck* are we gonna get out of here?" I asked. "There's gonna be some shit in here."

"No doubt," Dre said. "Man, go find out where the limo is."

The atmosphere was nutty. I walked outside and there were so many niggas. Just a sea of niggas. I could hear people talkin'.

"Fuck them Death Row niggas. We gon' fuck them niggas up."

Aw shit. But then, what does it say about our crew when we relished times like this? We lived on the absolute edge.

I saw the limo driver in front of the venue and told him, "Look here, man, don't you motherfuckin' move from this spot. You see me comin' you get that door open and get ready to get the fuck on up out of here!"

I walked back from the sidewalk and through the Garden entrance. Niggas was steady hollerin', "Fuck Death Row."

"Dre," I said once I waded back to my seat. The show was nearing its close. "I found the car, dog. But I'm-a let you know now—Them niggas is sayin' 'Fuck Death Row.' 'Fuck niggas.' 'Fuck it *all.*'

"There's gonna be some *shit*," I continued. "So nigga, keep movin' 'cuz we can't fight all them niggas, mayn. It ain't gon' happen."

We took off when the last award was handed out. *Whoosh!*

We got outside and niggas was cool—at first. Then they saw Dre. The threats started.

"Whuttup Dre!" They were tryin' to make us break stride.

"Aw, that nigga Dre cool . . ." I heard someone say.

This was a good sign. Not that we didn't like drama, but looking around it was impossible to like the odds.

"Yeah . . . But fuck them otha niggas, though!"

Aw shit.

We got away that night, although a blind man could see this was the beginning of something, not the end of anything.

Suge made a huge splash in the world of rap magazines and with hungry, unsigned rappers around southern California. And as the rivalry with Puffy's Bad Boy records got bigger, he got larger than life. Suge liked the limelight as much as he craved money. Who knew? I'd soon learn there was someone even heavier on the scene than a 315-lb.-Blood with Academic All-American football status from the University of Nevada-Las Vegas.

When I first met Jimmy Iovine, Interscope president and the only man on the scene heavier than Suge, I didn't truly understand who he was. To me, he was just a short white guy who rolled up on the Interscope offices in a Beamer, a dude whose ways were pretty bossy. And I knew he was the man with the money.

Jimmy got on back in the 1970s, when he produced the great Patti Smith song, "Because the Night." It was Jimmy on his Jersey shit, producing this punk writer chick doing a Springsteen song. That's all you need to know about that dude. He's an old-school Jersey guy. Jumped in the game as Springsteen's engineer. Little engineer motherfucker with a baseball cap on. Smartest motherfucker in the room.

Interscope was formed seven years earlier by Iovine and Marshall

Field's heir Ted Field with cash backing from Atlantic Records (which owned half the stock in the label). In time the label would boast of having Nine Inch Nails and No Doubt in addition to Death Row's artists. Industry vets used to talk about Jimmy at Ted's house begging for money, back before Death Row was even a fully formed idea. But Jimmy and Ted had this company, and it was initially distributed by Atlantic Records' subsidiary East-West Records. Like every other label before it, Interscope sent a guy to get the music and another nigga to get the money. Guess where Marshall Field's boy went? It wasn't a studio.

Jimmy was good with music. Back then it didn't really matter that the boss didn't know or seem to particularly love his hip-hop assignment. And that's all our shit was to him, the rap assignment. This nigga Jimmy wanted dollars. Wasn't a whole bunch of art for art's sake about to be goin' on. Not with the rap music, not at this stage of his career.

When I first met the big man at Interscope, he didn't seem to take special notice, which didn't much bother me because I knew I was the new cat. But from watching him interact further with other members of the Death Row camp, I quickly began to feel that he didn't consider me any different from the average kid Suge might drag in from off the avenue. The way our relationship played out definitely reinforced those early feelings. In time it would become clear that his M.O. would be seek control over Dre by getting control over me.

And Jimmy and Suge did take turns controlling Dre. I could see this early on, but I didn't say a whole lot. I was just the new guy. Jimmy always tried to have Dre under his wing and Suge always wanted to have Dre under his wing. Whoever had allegiance of the hitmaker would win.

The problem with Suge is he didn't just aim to be king of the music industry. He wanted to rule in the streets as well.

Around Christmas 1996, as Dre and his girl and me and my girl were sitting in a Pico penthouse, Dre came up with the idea of finishing up the night in the Hollywood Hills. He thought we should check out the Death Row holiday party.

We got to the spot and it was not a good look. It was a straight-up hoodrat convention. All the top-shelf drinks were on the second level, so we get to steppin', but we heard some odd noises as we got to the top of the stairs. And who revealed himself but Suge, clearing everyone out of the room.

"Dre, you and Bruce are good, but everyone else: Out!"

In comes Tupac with Suge's boys and a dude from Puffy's camp. Tensions had risen even higher since *The Source* Awards. Tupac was accusing Biggie of having set him up and shot prior to his prison stint. For his part, Biggie put out the ambiguous underground single "Who Shot Ya?" 'Pac responded by saying he had banged Big's wife, Faith Evans, on the song "Hit 'Em Up" and in other media. It was a hectic time, so if you're in Puffy's camp, why be at a Death Row party? This is at the height of battle, because Big Jake Robles, Suge's bodyguard, had just gotten killed at Jermaine Dupri's party in Atlanta. So Puffy's man's presence was taken like a 'fuck you.' It was like, "I'm in yo' shit! *What!?!*"

They sat the dude down in the chair and just started punchin' him in the grill. *Blam, blam, blam.*

"Where's Puffy's mom live?" Suge asked.

Dre and I had walked in on some shit we didn't need to be around. Same shit, different toilet.

Tupac wasn't sayin' nothin'. None of us were.

I noticed that this cat looked jumpy, like he was going to make a move. There was someone guarding the door and the only way out was the window. Now, if this dude tries something dumb, Dre and I are fucked.

I can only guess why, but Suge gives the dude—whose mouth is a bloody mess—some expensive-ass champagne. As a matter of reflex, he spit it out onto the floor.

Suge goes, "You spit out this good shit I gave you?" He's dead up in the kid's face, scaring the shit out of him.

And the guy jumps up and heads for the window.

Dre looked at me and I could tell his thoughts reflected my own: *Oh shit! If this cat gets out the window, we all in court.* Dre don't need this and neither do I. As the dude leaped toward the window, I caught him just before he smashed the glass. Suge let him walk away, like a walking advertisement for his attack skills.

I saw him at a party a few years later. He looked at me like the episode had never happened. Maybe he had just been in too much shock on that night in the Hollywood Hills.

Just before all of this, *Vibe* magazine organized a summit of artists and producers with political and business leaders. It took place in a Manhattan hotel ballroom and included key parties in the Bad Boy and Death Row beef, as well as *Vibe* founder Quincy Jones, *Black Enterprise* publisher Earl Graves, and Colin Powell. Their general message to the music industry people in attendance?

"Yo: come get with us and let us show you how to use that power and that money!"

They saw that we were gathering an enormous amount of clout, and they wanted in. It always seemed these leaders flaunted an opportunistic energy. You never saw these Negroes on the ground floor of some hip-hop endeavor. And those meetings that Farrakhan calls? I'm not usually one to knock the next man's hustle, but obviously the guise is black unity and ending black-on-black whatever whatever. Usually in a half-assed way. (Anybody remember the *Million Man March* album? A lot of talented artists contributed a lot of good songs, and the Nation of Islam had no idea how to get that music to a rabid collection of consumers.) Compilation tapes are fine, I guess. Everybody's tryin' to get paid. But don't just treat us like some suckas who are gonna bow down at the simple insistence that we come get with you.

These guys' whole take was, hey, y'all don' fucked around and got all this power and now you're wildin' out, actin' crazy. These were the voices of our prestigious "older heads," our leaders. And they acted as though they thought we were dumb. Did they think all this money and all this music just up and made itself? I found most of the talk insulting.

There wasn't a moment in this day-long conference where they offered up a single meaningful solution. Colin Powell gave a speech about how he'd been talking to a group of kids. Be strong, stay in school, Powell told them. Listen to your parents and be a better man. One kid stood up and told Powell that he felt he could grow up to be as great as Powell, except that he didn't have parents who supported him. The kid asked the question: "Would you have made it so far without parents that supported you?" It was the realest thing that got said all day. The general was stopped dead in his tracks. He said the boy's words hurt him like a knife, and he admitted he had no answer.

No one does. That's why shit can get so hectic with black youth. It's why they need hip hop, the only thing that allows them to come up off the bottom of society without asking that they miraculously change.

Hell yeah, there was beef. But the bottom line is that these leaders didn't know what to do. If you're tellin' everybody what they should do and how they should act, but you don't know what a dude's personal hell is when he wakes up and he can't even get a meal, what good are you?

All that money and power gathered together and not a single useful answer. Pathetic.

Big Jake Robles, the soon-to-be-departed bodyguard and a great, gentle giant, asked the bigwigs to consider the reasons people kill. He pointed out that at some point in life with no money, no opportunity, you'll be like, "I don't want to feel nuthin', I don't want to do nuthin'." And as time passes, you get hungry. And your kids get hungry. And that's when it gets crazy. Pretty soon you're backed into a corner and are gonna be like, you know what? I'm either gonna die or I'm-a be like, fuck it.

No doubt, there were negative things in the hip-hop community that were happening—with crews fighting each other, diss records goin' back and forth—that made these leaders look at us like we were some stupid-ass niggas wildin' out. Obviously inside each crew you had more than some knuckleheads who did stupid shit. But most of us were struggling to keep our crews and business arrangements together. There was money, but not a lot of brothas prepared to lead. Throughout the history of rap, plenty of crews have risen and fallen.

If you're a rapper or whatever you try to pick the right cats to come up with you. That's the difference between it and pro sports. In that game it's understood that the players leave their old friends behind. The separation is almost mandatory. In hip hop these people have never left the streets. No other entertainment is so connected to the streets. That's the strength of hip hop, but the street quality—which for some reason human beings can't get enough of—comes with a price tag.

Say you're a hip-hop artist, comin' from the streets, and you got your street niggas with you, and you blow up. When you go back to your projects or your 'hood there's other niggas that you *ain't* with, that you *ain't* grow up with, that *ain't* your homeboys. They're lookin' at you funny, almost hungrily. So you can't roll by yourself. Having a posse is all but contractually obligated for a hip-hop artist. It's a matter of security as much as it's about keeping things real.

They say don't leave the 'hood. But, okay, let's say you make somethin'. You build a house in the 'hood, the property values suck. You ain't even gonna get what you put into it. And then there's gonna be some knucklehead who's gonna try to rob you. So, you got to get out.

For a rapper, it don't matter whether he gets out or not. He's still got to be close to the 'hood. It don't matter. He's connected. He's gonna have to deal with the drama, some way, somehow. If he's gotta have niggas with him, he's gotta have niggas with him. And if he's gotta have niggas with him for some street thing, how is he gonna say,

Humble beginnings
Bruce's grandmother's house in Bunkie, LA.
Bruce Williams Collection

The good ol' days
(From left) Uncle David, DJ, and Bruce
deer hunting in Bunkie.
Bruce Williams Collection

Serious weaponry
Bruce at basic training (Fort Benning, GA).
Bruce Williams Collection

One cool Army dude
Bruce in uniform.
Bruce Williams Collection

Taking direction
(From left) Ice Cube, F. Gary Gray, and Dre on the set with a production crew.
Bruce Williams Collection

Chris Tucker holding court
(From left) Ice Cube, Mohammed, Chris Tucker, and
Bruce cracking jokes with others.
Bruce Williams Collection

Rapper of all trades.
Mack 10 giving Ice Cube a shape-up.
Bruce Williams Collection

Pac in thought
Tupac at Dre video shoot.
Bruce Williams Collection

The night life
Dre and Bruce at a dinner party at
Transatlantic in downtown Los Angeles.
Vivian Williams

Calabasas living

(From left) Bruce (white T-shirt), Big Tiny, Dre, Big Bruce, and others at
Dre's birthday party (Dre's house, Calabasas, CA).

Bruce Williams Collection

Freestyling

(From left) J. Flex (writer, *Keep Your Head Up* and *Been There, Done That*),
Snoop Dogg, Dre (background), and B'uddah (producer, Aftermath).
At Dre's house parties everyone gets on the mic!

Bruce Williams Collection

Shooting dice
(Clockwise from left) Unidentified man, Tracy Jones, Snoop Dogg,
Kurupt, and Warren G around Dre's pool table.
Bruce Williams Collection

Aftermath's Man of the Decade
The crew honors Dre with the Aftermath Man of the
Decade Award (Bruce in the background).
Bruce Williams Collection

How we do
Dre and Bruce at Aftermath boat
party for the whole crew.
Vivian Williams

"Ain't Nuthin' But a 'G' Thang"
Snoop and Dre onstage at the Up in Smoke Tour.
Richard Segal Huredia

Officer Cooper
Eminem messing around on a video shoot.
Richard Segal Huredia

The end of an era
(From left) Melman, Mike, Dre, Bruce, and J-Boogie
on our last trip to Vegas as a crew.
Bruce Williams Collection

The doctor operating
Dre and Bruce on the
boards, Can Am Studios.
Richard Segal Huredia

Legends
The late, great Roger Troutman and
Dre at the recording session for
"Five Minutes to Flush," at
Record One studio.
Richard Segal Huredia

Focus
Dre and Sam Sneed at work in the Larrabee West studio.
Richard Segal Huredia

Masterpiece in progress
D.O.C. writing lyrics,
Sierra Sonic studios.
Richard Segal Huredia

Life on the other side
Dre behind the mic,
"one lip up" attitude. Sierra
Sonic studios in Reno, NV,
recording "Still D.R.E.,"
The Chronic album.
Richard Segal Huredia

Working for flawlessness
Eve and Dre perfecting it
at Encore studio. First
session with Eve.
Richard Segal Huredia

Until it's right
(From left) Hitman,
Richard (engineer),
Dre, and Snoop
working in the Larrabee
West studio, studio A,
mixing *The Chronic*
album.
Richard Segal Huredia

Perfectionists at work
Eminem writing,
Dre behind the boards at
Sierra Sonic studios,
Reno, NV.
Richard Segal Huredia

Dedication
Ice Cube fine-tuning lyrics with Dre.
Encore studio, Burbank,
CA, N.W.A. Reunion.
Richard Segal Huredia

"What U See Is What U Get"
Xzibit and Eminem at the
Larrabee West studio, studio A.
Richard Segal Huredia

"No Diggity"
Chauncey Black,
Teddy Riley, Jimmy Iovine,
and Dre at a session,
Can Am Studios' backroom.
Richard Segal Huredia

Studio cipher
D.O.C., Snoop, Warren G, and Nate Dogg talking shop at Encore studio.
Richard Segal Huredia

"Some L.A. N*az"**
MC Ren and Dre,
Larrabee North, studio A.
Richard Segal Huredia

Dre's wedding day
Bruce, Bruce Wheatley,
Dre, and Larry C. at
Dre's wedding in Maui.
Vivian Williams

Modern-day Mozart
Dre serenading
Bruce and Vivian.
Bruce Williams Collection

Here and now
Vivian and Bruce at
their wedding.
Bruce Williams Collection

The best man
Bruce and Dre walking to
the altar at Bruce's wedding.
Bruce Williams Collection

Making it legit

Dre signs the marriage license at Bruce's wedding.

Bruce Williams Collection

Army Aces

John West and Bruce at Bruce's wedding.

Bruce Williams Collection

Young Shark
Sir B Williams, age 8.
Bruce Williams Collection

Spring Training
Mister Williams, age 5.
Bruce Williams Collection

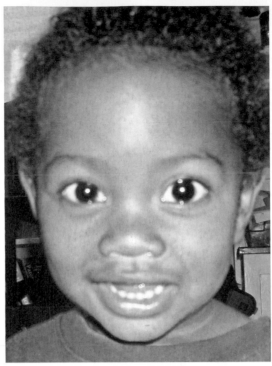

Pretty brown eyes
Prince Williams, age 16 months.
Bruce Williams Collection

Giving back
(Clockwise from right) Melman, Bruce, and Harris at a South Africa HIV Center,
where all residents are carriers of HIV
Bruce Williams Collection

"Oh, I'm going to this awards show now. You can't come." How is he gonna tell them that? Them niggas gon' be like, "Oh, he on that bull-shit."

The trouble is built in. I'll tell you what, though: Hip hop did something that no one thought it was gonna do. And it wasn't just white people who didn't know what it was gonna do, it was actually black people, too. I mean the *Vibe* conference attendees were just sittin' in this room, in that meeting, and they didn't realize the music, the culture, and the fashion were gonna get so big. Maybe if they really did understand our potential, these people could have proposed a meaningful partnership with us. They didn't realize the money was gonna get that big, that the power was gonna get that high. Maybe if they did, they would have come around at times that weren't troubled, times when we appeared vulnerable. They probably thought it was time to get in on it before the thing faded away. That's about how fair-weather these people—with the exception of Quincy Jones—seemed to me.

At one point, Suge stood up and asked everyone in the room, "While I'm here, can y'all sign my petition against everyone who is condemning our music and going against our company?" He was talking about C. Delores Tucker and those pressuring Time Warner and the other major labels to give up hard core rap music. And don't you know he didn't get a single signature?

If they were to have that event today, how would they come at us differently? There's nothing they can really do at this point. What's the real problem right now? About all you can say is "I really don't like the words." I mean, how many kids are getting beat up in the streets over hip hop right now? Who's dying in rap music now?

You don't see that on the news every day anymore. I mean, think about it: About all you hear is that 50 Cent got stopped in his Ferrari, and he didn't have no license, didn't have no insurance. It's the ballplayers now who get most of big ugly headlines. And those cats are actually well behaved, well reared. It says something about what causes trouble, music or the streets. It's gotta be the latter because, as that Brooklyn cat Dre collaborates with said, the streets is watchin'.

No way. The problem is not and never was hip hop. It's not at all that simple.

Chapter Ten

Darling Nikki

Because of my relationship with Dre, I was the first to notice he was withdrawing a little bit from the scene. It was noticeable only if you were looking closely—fewer production credits on this one, then that one; less of a presence in the Death Row club entourage. The good Doctor was definitely stepping back, and for an understandable reason. There were starting to be more cats in the studio who he ain't really know. They were telling him he was supposed to make their records. The vibe around Death Row was getting funny. You were starting to see more records produced by niggas other than Dre.

Dre's withdrawal didn't really have to do with Death Row, at the end of the day. It was Eazy that helped get him out of harm's way. Dre said time and again how he couldn't get over the sight of Eazy, someone he'd grown up in the streets with, lyin' lifeless—outta the blue. Eric Wright's death brought back the realness. A lot of these other cats might get lost in the Hollywood glare, but he wasn't gonna be one of them.

The way Eazy died fueled the "Dre is gay" rumors. We found that phenomenon ridiculous. Eazy was known as "The Bareback Champ" because of how he got down with women. It wasn't from fuckin' dudes. Nobody from our camp listened to the rumors, and we never retaliated against those who originated or passed on the notion. Still, there's no question Eazy's death played a role in Dre's decision to get married. He might not ever admit it, but he was in a more restless state than usual when he linked up with the woman who would change his entire world.

At that time Emilio Estevez and Paula Abdul were married and living next to a second crib that I once rented for Dre in Malibu. Day in, day out, we threw parties, right there on the beach. We had the Pacific Ocean in our frontyard. All of the pretty girls from Hollywood and around started coming to our functions. Why wouldn't they? Our parties were the kind that, when you stepped in the door I'd hand you a joint that was no fucking joke and I'd light it. Then you'd kick it like you were livin' the videos, minus the drama.

The girls who steadily attended the Malibu functions were stupid hot, even for my high Hollywood-bred standards. This woman named Nicole was at one particular party with another function regular named Acana and a bunch of other light-skinned girls. And they were just tryin' to talk, talk, talk—nonconsequential chatter with no clear payoff. (Check, please!) I wasn't feelin' them like *that,* so I politely took their numbers and stepped off.

I remember it clearly. On a Thursday afternoon right after that Malibu joint, Dre called me.

"Whassup?" he asked.

"What's happenin', man? I'm chillin', just workin' on some bullshit. What's up?"

"Man, let's go to Vegas!"

"Vegas?"

"Tomorrow! Yeah, let's go!" Young Dre was an impulsive cat.

"Tomorrow? Well, who all's goin'? Let me see if I can set the shit up."

Dre hung up. Before I could figure out a strategy, he rang me again.

"Hey, man. Let's take some bitches."

"Aiight."

I hung up and started to think about who I could take to Vegas on such short notice. Like I said, our standards had become pretty high at this point. We definitely weren't tryin' to take a bunch of hoodrats to party. There were rules against shit like that. So I called up Acana from the Malibu party. That girl looked good, wasn't a dummy, and seemed down to have a good time. She was like, "Yeah, I'm-a go witcha!"

Nicole was there. I could hear her in the background. *I wanna go! I wanna go!*

"My friend Nicole wants to go."

"Fuck all that," I said. "I only got one ticket. You coming or not. I don't know about your friend."

"No, no, no. I wanna go."

"Cool. I'll hit you back and tell you what's up."

Then I get a call from Dre.

"I need some new girls, man. *You* got some girls. Man, come on."

This probably meant Dre had fallen out with one of the countless chicks he had run through since breaking up with Michel'le. No question, we all went through a lot of women. It could feel like a competition sometimes, and Dre set the bar pretty high. Being a star gave him advantages that none of us could contend with.

"Man, I ain't got no chicks," I said, maybe as a reflex. My inclination was to say that chicks keep themselves, but of course I kept a roster of women. I wasn't that much into sharing, though. "Hold up . . . Let me call you right back."

I called Acana.

"Your friend still there?"

"Nicole?"

"Yeah," she replied. "Let me put her on."

I wasted little precious time. The invite was just another thing on my morning things-to-do list. I should have thought twice. Maybe I should have thought thrice.

"Nicole, what's up? Wanna go to Vegas?"

"Yeah!"

Then she asked, "Who's your homeboy?"

"You know who it is. Dre."

"Well, that's alright," she said without a second's hesitation.

I told Dre that I'd found someone who wanted to go to Vegas with him. We didn't usually take women on our trips to that desert city.

"I'm-a go pick up the girls then come back and get you, 'cuz your ass takes too long to get ready," I said. Maybe it was because he grew up with a single mother who scrimped every day to get him looking nice, but he seriously fussed over his appearance. On top of that, he got distracted by music—his own and that of others. He might play a hot new song ten times in a row and end up an hour off schedule. I'd stop by his apartment at The Argon all rushed, and my buzz would be seriously harshed.

"You ain't gonna make us late this time, nigga," I warned, jokingly.

I scooped the girls and had the limo take us back to pick up Dre. He was all lookin' in the window to check out his new traveling companion.

"Which one is mine?"

I motioned to Nicole.

He looked at her and gave me a thumbs-up.

We rolled out and the rest is history. What I thought was supposed to be a hookup had her livin' next door to Dre a week and a half later. And she's been around ever since.

Dre and Nicole took me to dinner not so long after they became inseparable. I think Dre was drawn to her because Nicole is aggressive and talks a lot of smack, just like his favorite MCs. But, personally, I never truly understood what Dre saw in this woman. She's the kind of person who has to be first, with everyone else following her lead. You simply have to do what she wants to do. Everyone and everything would have to be under her. In time, a bunch of us who watched the relationship bloom would come to call Nicole by the nickname Corleone.

Individually, they could both be astoundingly full of shit, so maybe it was natural for them to be a good couple.

On this night, Nicole's skinny, pretty ass seemed to be smiling a little bit more than usual. There were drinks on the table, and the food was coming. Dre's mood seemed especially serious that night. It was obvious he had something big to tell me.

"Yo," Dre said, pausing to look over at his girl, "Me and Nicole is getting ready to tie the knot."

That came a little out of left field. It had been a whirlwind courtship. I wasn't really with that marriage shit, but I told him, "Hey, congratulations."

"Actually," Dre interrupted, "I want you to be my best man."

You don't want The D.O.C. to be your best man? I asked myself, incredulous. The D.O.C. had been through hell and high water with Dre. Didn't he ask him?

Naw. He wanted me.

I was overwhelmed. No words would come out of my mouth. My reaction must have looked crazy to them.

Even though I'm authoritative and been in the military, I'm still a sensitive cat. So, my friend's question this night just blew me away. It was deep. Here was this prolific producer, a musical genius, and he was asking *me* to be his best man. There were just so many people Dre could have chosen. A part of me had felt like I was merely his work buddy.

In the craziness of our rap music lives, we *were* best friends and all that, but we never really talked heartfelt on a regular basis. This request felt like a whole different level of responsibility, like our relationship was deeper than just work and friends. The whole impact of what Dre asked simply shut me down.

The woman he was about to marry looked at me quizzically.

"That doesn't make you happy?" Nicole said. "Aren't you surprised? Aren't you excited?"

I don't think she was hip that, from an emotional standpoint, Dre had me on the floor. A person like her couldn't imagine where I was coming from. It's like: The D.O.C. is an amazing, one-of-a-kind motherfucker; together he and Dre went through it all. Warren G and Doc go back almost their whole lives. Chris Tucker was a good friend. And out of all the niggas in Hollywood, this cat asked me. That meant what we'd gone through really was more than work. Dudes don't really talk about being best friends, but Dr. Dre and I were. And this confirmation was seriously dope. Finally, I felt, I had concrete family.

"Bruce?" Dre prodded me for a response, interrupting my thoughts.

"Yeah," I said, to both of them, finally. "I'm happy."

We drank a toast and then chatted about a big wedding of the sort people would talk about for years.

The wedding was, of course, a beautiful thing. But instead of the spectacle we had talked about with so much enthusiasm, Dre and Nicole decided to go small. They invited just a few friends and family to gather at the Four Seasons in Maui. The Pacific Ocean was the backdrop.

For some reason the wedding doesn't stick in my mind as much as that night at dinner. The way Nicole seemed confused by my stunned silence, the expression on Dre's face when I said yes. Mostly I remember thinking before, during, and after we toasted, that I wasn't even supposed to be here. I'd done okay for a country boy who had strayed so far.

Nicole, who hailed from Seattle, showed Dre a lot beyond music and Compton and the things one sees while promoting and making albums. Shit like nature and high culture and whatnot. She showed him a level of contentedness he couldn't have imagined. He really did become that different man the death of Eazy made him want to be. A part of me, however, wished I'd never made those calls that night for the Vegas trip. Was it really good to be content and edgeless in the kind of shark tank that was our everyday domain?

Chapter Eleven

Giving Suge His Due

In my gut I feel something funny about the way Tupac died with Suge that September night in Vegas. I just don't see how all these hard-core niggas who had been around Suge and 'Pac all that time—always packin' heat—could let a car dump on them, in a lot of traffic, and *no one* got one shot at the assailants. Death Row security had been way too thorough for that. It had come so far since putting Snoop in that Blood neighborhood during that early video shoot. After the Tyson fight, out on that main drag, Suge shouldn't have been so off guard. No one got a shot off? I just find that kinda fishy.

'Pac had just fired his lawyer, David Kenner, who was also Death Row's official attorney. This move signaled to some that 'Pac was about to make a move off the label. When you fire your attorney, who is also your company's attorney, something is about to jump off.

I'm just lookin' at the facts. This dude was getting ready to leave the label and gets called up to Vegas for the fight. He wears his bullet-proof (right?) vest everywhere and yet on this occasion he happens to not have it on. This is just one black man's opinion, and all I can do is speculate. But the whole thing seems kind of fishy to me.

You gotta understand, 'Pac was gettin' ready to go; he was fixin' to leave Death Row. Why do you think he did all those albums? He would say shit like, "Man, I done sold all these fuckin' albums; how I still owe this nigga?" Suge had Tupac's deal set up so that he could never re-coup his advances. Plus, 'Pac was messin' with Quincy Jones's daugh-ter, Kidadda. Quincy was talking to him about getting his business straight and his life together and realizing his untapped potential. Quincy saw that he could do great things. Suge had to be wondering about the prospect of yet another meal ticket leaving, this time for Jones and Warner Bros.

There was a time when people thought I got killed, because there was this other cat who got killed whose name was Bruce. This Bruce had put hands on Suge. Suge was talkin' shit and the dude was nice with his hands. It was like *wop-pop*—and Suge got dropped. That made him look bad. He's supposed to be all Mr. Toughy-Toughy, and he got knocked on his back by this cat Bruce. So Suge did things his way: later on he went and got street on this motherfucker. Suge and his boys went over to Bruce's workplace to start some shit, and Suge got dropped again. Bruce had quick, strong hands.

A couple of months later, word got around that Bruce got shot in the head.

Right after that, people were like, "Bruce, I heard you got killed."

"That wasn't fuckin' me, man!"

But because I was in that scene, and I was in good shape, and I had stood up to Suge before, people assumed it was me who had the squabble with Suge. Hell, no! I might be a humble country boy, but I'm not dumb enough to fuck with Suge like *that*.

After that Suge would always tell me war stories. And I could never figure out why, because that type of shit didn't interest me. We did this, we did that. We hit this dude, we squashed that . . .

But all in all, Suge was a cool-ass dude. He just went overboard. Dre always said, "The one who you least expect is the one who'll mostly do things." When Suge got Dre out of his unfair Ruthless Records deal, he was that dude. When he got Interscope to distribute Death Row? He was that dude. Roughly the time of *The Source* Awards Suge stopped being that dude.

. . .

Here's something controversial: Jerry Heller had it right. Remember that manager Eric Wright went into business with to start Ruthless Records? That motherfucker got it dead right when he said Suge had an intimidating presence. Suge started as a security guard at Ruthless, next thing you know he's taking the primary talent away. The Ruthless people weren't random losers, but they let Suge get the drop on them.

More than a bat, the guy had wiles, ambition, and charm. Who else, aside from Heller, could have come between Dre and Eazy?

But Dre and Suge did big things. They helped make street thug music the soundtrack of choice for America's youth. Tupac posters on little white girls' bedroom walls was at least as shocking as Elvis gyrating on *The Ed Sullivan Show*. As we witnessed the strength of street knowledge, the music spread. Grandmaster Kaz to Schoolly D to N.W.A. and then the international explosion. Puff Daddy committed to producing gangsta-inflected pop. Def Jam snatched up DMX. Seeds down south. Atlanta, New Orleans, and Miami were coming into their own. The music turned worldwide. Hip hop in Paris is now gangsta. My friend the director Mathieu Kassovitz (he directed *Gothika*) told me that he learned English primarily by listening to N.W.A. and Ice-T records. And Thug Life lives in Africa. It's crazy how this "negative" music can bring people together.

In the wake of all the crackdowns on hip hop that have emerged over recent years—and they are really just the same lick that privileged people have been hitting since it was decided black music (even black people, if you wanna get super-real) were forces to be controlled—you gotta think about who criticizes the music. It's everybody but those who are supposedly affected by the music. Only the players within that subset have changed. Now you got Oprah and Al Sharpton in the mix. That's the only muthafuckin' difference.

Nobody even gives a damn about freedom of speech. It's all just lip service. If Americans really are allowed to say what they want to say, then let them say what they want to say. And if what someone says doesn't agree with you, then speak your piece and move on. People will forget about the words and the situation will defuse itself, eventually. It's crazy to harp on things.

As a guy who's been in the hip-hop game, at the top of the game, for so, so many years, I sit back and listen to Oprah have her little conversations with Russell Simmons and other representatives of hip hop along with the gender and race activists with a little bit of skepticism. Nobody really responds to what I think is the crucial issue.

And that's this: Who designated "bitches" and "hos" to black women only? Black women—the ones who can get on TV—stand up like we're just talking about them and that's not at all what we're talking about.

If people are gonna say hip hop isn't just entertainment anymore—and we in hip hop are insisting the opposite—okay, let's go there. Hip hop is real then, and we only write and rap about what we see. Let's play along:

I've been there, city to city all over America. There are girls that will run up to you, accost you *just because you have a laminate on your neck*. And I'm not even a star! Doesn't matter. You could have a laminate on your neck, be the lowest peon in the group—not even actually be in the group. And hear this:

"I'll do *anything* to get backstage with you."

And women wanna act like this isn't a part of who they are as females in America? Is there some sort of mass allergy to the truth? Why can't we just admit this? And what are we supposed to call this?

Here is where nasty blow jobs are born.

One of the reasons that raps about pimps and hos—a subset of that great new American storytelling tradition, the gangsta narrative, like *The Sopranos*—sell so well is that prostitution is woven into the fabric of post–World War II Western culture. There's a little bit of ho in Princess Di, a little bit of ho in Hillary. We know, yet won't honestly talk, about how their celebrity and proximity to fame helped them get what they want. Now, this doesn't make 'em bad. It does make 'em hos, though.

And for black women to say that we're only talking about them, well, that's an ignorance that's born of presumption. If, as we're just alleging here, rappers only write about what they see, then we have to be talking about *all* women. Not just the sistas. In those tour situations, it's mostly white women. So, don't be so quick to take the prostitute stigma on as your own.

Maybe these critical black women just don't want to acknowledge the possibility that we're not talking about them.

I've been out there and watched literally thousands of women sing those songs that TV-ready activists criticize. Historically, women have bought the majority of recorded music. And I've seen them sing those songs word for word—and be glad about it! *It ain't no fun if the homies can't have none!* Now, that might not be your trip, but for some females of the human species it is. These women find that form of sexuality gratifying, if only for a time. (And, believe me, they are appreciated.)

I've heard women refer to themselves in these terms: Yeah, I'm a bitch! I'm a ho! And I'd be like, *Daayymm,* you that hard core widdit? Yeeeah!

So, it's like this is stuff that actually goes on in the world—a lot. Maybe it's time to start talking to the women for a minute. I've got sons out there, and I don't want things to be too crazy out there when it's time for them to get with these wild girls. It might be hard for you to hear, comin' from someone who helped Dr. Dre's music get into the world so deep, but take responsibility and teach your kids what's going on.

Dre produced Eminem, but he doesn't let his young children hear it.

Sex and violence has been sellin' even before hip hop was invented. If you've ever seen *Cribs,* you know that the honorary god of hip-hop culture is Al Pacino as Tony Montana from *Scarface*. Everybody has that poster or painting or T-shirt in their possession. Why isn't anyone ever up pointing in the face of the film's director Brian DePalma or Oliver Stone, who wrote the flick? Why is no one ever trying to ban *Scarface*?

Tony Montana works for the same reason that Tony Soprano resonates and Michael Corleone resonates: Because it's hella fuckin' gangsta out in the world, on the corner, on Wall Street and in Baghdad. It's gotten to the point with the way the world is today that cowboys and Indians just don't cut it no mo'. (Although the notion that the pioneers get all the arrows while the settlers are the ones who get the land still holds up remarkably well.) Shit, real life reveals cowboys and Indians paradigm to be the fairy tale that it actually is. People need gangsta. The old shit just ain't cuttin' it no mo'.

People who don't care about gangsta music should just not listen to it. To censor recording artists is no better than burning books. It takes a black man who's struggled and literally fought to get away from the streets and says, "No, what you're speaking on is not legit." It deprives him of his one way. Unless you're Will Smith, most people don't want to hear your raps about fatherhood, as important as being a good dad is. LL Cool J made a song in 2006 and couldn't even get it played on the radio.

So what does that say about our culture of entertainment? The cable "news" channels—not really news, just a show about current events—features this month's murder story line or this week's famous sex hoochie story line. And you can't get songs about family much airplay. I don't really know the meaning of this, except that if we could actually pay the radio stations enough, they might air those kinds of songs. That says a lot about how alive our culture of pimps and hos really is. And if you think about it, the hip-hop artists are far from the pimps in this scenario.

You'd get a record company owner, not someone smart like a Clive Davis or an Iovine, who's like, "Yo, that shit over there is hot. I need some of that shit." These are the copycats. They take an artist and force the kid to be something that he's not. That's when producers take aside an artist already under him and tell the kid: I know who you are. But I'm gonna need you to give me a little bit of this, too, now. And God forbid this cat don't sell and has to take his broke ass back to Kansas City or wherever. They play with dudes' lives.

This is why radio programmers have a near monopoly on clout as I write this book. Everybody who wants to even be *in* the game has to make a radio hit. Now you gotta pay stations to get your record on the air—and they're only gonna play the same sort of rap music anyway.

Most important to this West Coast music movement, it got people into the media game. Directors, fashion people, writers, etc. (Every time some politician complained about how he cleaned up his city in the late nineties, all I ever thought was, Don't credit Guiliani, credit Jay-Z. Hip hop did more to get street niggas into corporate spaces than R.I.F. and a hundred internships.) This was the music of the people who were not interested in waiting for government handouts or for the rules of succeeding in society to be bent toward our black asses.

A part of me feels like Suge stupidly ruined everything, assuming Death Row's business model was ever truly tenable in the first place, but he had us doin' L.A. gangsta shit, bastard of Black Panthers–type shit, and doin' it *big*. The whole world walks a little more like a raw-ass southern California nigga now, and that's some deep, deep shit. Death Row went for it, went out guns a-blazing, but I can't be mad at it. That's hip hop. It takes a toll. And, anyway, if I am mad at it, there's a few billion motherfuckers over in Asia who *will* make their peace with it. What we have created has worldwide utility like that. People inevitably will do what they want with hip hop, hate it or love it. I'm just giving advice. The music itself cannot be stopped.

To me, Suge was a good business cat—you wouldn't think it because of his thug life, but he was a smart businessman. Dre needed him for the business end of things. Dre did music, and that's what he loved. He didn't love the business part of it. Suge did. And that's why they made a good team and made shit work.

Here's how smart a businessman Suge was *before* he started having an image to uphold:

The soundtrack for New Line's *Above the Rim*—which starred Tupac, before he signed with Death Row—was in development. This was even before *The Chronic* had become gigantic, when the label was still just getting started. The film's producers—who, like Interscope, had Time Warner money in it—came to the label and asked if Death Row would do a song for the soundtrack. Before the end of the day, Suge's like, "Why should we do a song *for* the soundtrack when we can do the *whole* soundtrack on our label?"

Fuck, by the close of business that day, that soundtrack was a Death Row project. It's industry lore how the early Suge would go get things done. Suge would figure out a way.

He came back to my boss like, "Dre, I got us a couple of million. We ain't gotta pay it back. I made Jimmy give it to us as a loan. We just ain't gotta pay it back."

Jimmy's tactic was to keep so many projects coming at Andre Young and from different angles that Dre couldn't completely focus on his own work. He'd just sort of go along with the program.' My friend knew that Jimmy couldn't make a good portion of his projects go without a Dre track. Yet, in the end, it was a no-brainer. Big-ticket industry distractions vs. cops at your door? Walking away from Death Row, an "L" that cost Dr. Dre millions initially, immediately changed the game.

As much as comfort lured Dre to write off Death Row as a starter business and cast his lot with Aftermath, it wasn't Jimmy's maneuverings that won out. It was the simple catastrophe of the streets interfering with business on Death Row. On the surface, the company, now in Beverly Hills at Wilshire and San Vicente Boulevards, resembled the great and burgeoning family business concern that so many civilians in L.A. came to see the place as. But if you looked at the core of things, street life had taken over. The thuggery had eaten Dre and Suge's entrepreneurial effort inside out.

Suge took to taking money from ballers in exchange for Dr. Dre beats. Then Suge wouldn't deliver. Just seeing so many local MCs get on at a national level, street hustlers began to feel that they could throw some money at some music and that would be it—they'd get an introduction to the top guys at the label and they'd be gone. As far as these cats were concerned, if they could get Dre to do a track for their artist, they were set. Suge encouraged this.

And Dre didn't know nothin' about these tracks he was supposed to be making. Suge had taken their money and walked off with it laughin', like, "Yeah. *Right,* motherfucka."

That's when Dre said enough was enough and he walked away. He wasn't having fun anymore. How could it be when thugs were acting like he owed them music. Every time he went to Can-Am, it would be somebody new sayin' "I'm signed to Death Row. You're supposed to do my album."

Suge signed these people, and he had a blind man's eye for talent. (Okay, he did snatch Tupac, but that guy was already on Interscope.) And Jeffrey Dahmer would have done a better job at managing relationships with rappers. Suge was smart at business in its most abstract, but when it came to cultivating talent he was terrible. Death Row never made a cent off an artist that Suge signed. To this day, he hasn't found a single artist who's made a hit. He didn't sign Snoop or Daz or Kurupt or Tupac or Nate Dogg. Give him credit for clearance cases like the crooner Danny Boy.

Chapter Twelve

Beyond Beef at Benihana

My best friend is complicated like a classical composer. That's why he would not come to court billionaire status as Sean Combs or Sean Carter. There's something about the guy that's reclusive. He's a true artist, with all the expected quirks.

I remember not too long ago, after all the Death Row madness, when we were in the studio and someone put on one of those cheesy novelty songs. You know the kind. Think "Pop, Drop and Lock It," but not really that. It was one of those songs that break through and become huge hits one or two times a year. Anyway, someone had put one of those shits on the system and as the tinny, cheap bars repeated ad infinitum, Busta started getting into it. He bopped around to the music. So did some of the cats in his crew. As Dre watched this, his expression turned sour.

"Y'all really like that shit?" he asked.

Hesitation filled the air. We all knew it wasn't the cup of tea for a maestro like Dre.

Busta said something to the effect of "Sure, what's wrong with a little distraction?" And his crew kept on bopping to the beat, just clownin'.

Well, Dre was quietly beside himself. He didn't say anything, but it was obvious to me. I saw that his production routine had morphed into something like pacing. He was there, but not quite there at all. In a matter of minutes, he'd gone from busy and in a groove to being a ghost among us.

Without anyone noticing, Dr. Dre slipped out the door. He didn't come back that day.

They were all like, "That's weird. Where did Dre go?" And no more songs got produced that day.

Up till now, I'm not sure if Busta and his crew know why he left. But *I* know. You gotta remember that Andre Young has a singular passion for the music we call hip hop. Once, back in 1983, he snuck into a punk rock club to see one of the first East Coast performances ever. This was even before Eve's After Dark opened its doors to the music. Dre has a hunger for the stuff in its purest form.

And he is touched and special. Now, Busta and his crew are uncommonly colorful people in their own right. Dr. Dre, however, is truly a different kind of cat.

In a way, Dre was lucky in that he'd been burned years back by Eazy-E and his Ruthless Records cohort Jerry Heller. My man wasn't going to make the same mistakes again. When the feds told us they were about to come down on Suge for conspiracy, the handwriting was on the wall. Dre signed away his portion of Death Row ownership— a move that would be ridiculed for years—and we were out the door. No business, no pleasure. Just tough talk and static from Suge and his soldiers.

Dre wasn't in the mix with local talent like he had been. And who could blame him? Too much drama. When not in the studio, he was mostly at home, getting into the role—finally—of family. Still, he tried to give young musicians solid advice. We were sitting in the living room of the Calabasas crib. Dre's place was a short shot from Can-Am, maybe six miles from the studio. Sam Sneed had been on his way to a meeting he'd been hastily informed of by a sketchy-sounding Death Row underling. He stopped along the way because something just didn't feel right to him.

We were telling Sam that he was right to trust his gut instinct.

"Sam," Dre told him, "you's a dumb muthafucka if you go to that meeting."

"Dude, don't go there," I cosigned. "You *know* what's about to go down."

But I could see he didn't know what to do. The kid from Pittsburgh was in a very fucked-up place. He had already been identified as too close to Dre and me. We were out and off the reservation. Despite— or perhaps because—Dre had opted to take an "L" on the business end of their partnership, Suge was calling Dre a faggot in the streets.

Suge's an interesting villain, but a little typical. You know what they say about people who point the "gay" finger most. Well, Suge did that more than anybody. And he bullied Puffy because Puffy *could* be punked. (Sean Combs was awkward around me; he got along with Dre, but seemed unclear on where I stood within the Death Row schism.) But he wouldn't bully them shadowy Italian types who were behind the label's attorney, David Kenner. (Shit, on the rare occasion that I rolled with him outside Los Angeles, Suge got out and started walking down an obscure Manhattan street with one of those heavy motherfuckers. There was such a scary aura to it. Man, I looked the other way, like I don't *want* to know!) Suge certainly wouldn't try bullying *real* street-connected niggas like gang activist Mike Conception or the mighty Big Wes or some of them other real, hard core cats. When dealing with them, he showed respect.

Regardless of what the dying Death Row was puttin' down, our core crew kept rollin'. Still Dre and me and Sam Sneed and The D.O.C. We were rollin', regardless. Everybody down at this point still really respected Dre. It was as if he were starting fresh all over, like MC Ren could come back again. Fresh, like Aftermath.

A lot of serious artists like B-Real and KRS-One were maneuvering behind the scenes to get on *Aftermath Presents,* Dr. Dre's new anthology, a little like that Tupac-era *Stowaways and Throwaways* collection. Only this time Dre would promote positive MCs. "Been

There, Done That," both Dre's and the album's first singles, rejected gangsta in a way that's painted him into a corner ever since.

"A million muthafuckas on the Planet Earth talk that hard bullshit 'cuz that's all they worth" spoke volumes. Dre was making a bold statement. And he was refreshed to learn that the hot young guns weren't completely turned off him by the Death Row chronicles. Anyway, Sam Sneed had a single in the chamber called "Recognize," his solo debut—a real hot one, too. But Dre had been to the video shoot—had seen who did cameos—and knew Suge wasn't calling a meeting with Sam just to confirm congratulations. Something just didn't feel right.

"Seriously, don't go to that meeting," I urged Sneed.

"You know we left Death Row," Dre chimed in. "You know them niggas know you wanna be with us. I just don't think it's a good idea."

Well, the kid wasn't trying to hear this. He was trying to be a stand-up guy. So he went out to Can-Am to screen that video.

It surprised Sneed that so many members of the family came out for this. Tupac was in the building, as were the usual complement of Suge's lackeys and even Hammer. The "Pumps and a Bump" gangsta makeover hadn't worked for the former multiplatinum rapper, but he was still hanging out. That seemed weird to Sneed. But nice, possibly. He wanted to believe it was recognition for the effort he had put into his product. Within weeks there was to be a Sam Sneed Death Row album in stores.

The stylized black-and-white footage rolled, and there was Dre rapping in close-up, just as expected. Negativity sucked the conference room empty, just as to be expected. Sam Sneed felt cause for concern, but he also thought they knew. Or maybe he thought they wouldn't care. It was, after all, a hella hecka tight video.

But the music sounded like a Death Row track, by which I mean it was a Dr. Dre track. And Dre was doing the hook. That was bad enough. Then the East Coast niggas started showing up in cameos. First some East Coast basketball cats, big and impressive names if you're from Brooklyn. This was the San Fernando Valley, though. And there was a war goin' on.

Tupac said, "If I see one more East Coast nigga in this mother-fucker . . ."

Sam had been flirting with a girl in the most dominant image of the video's second half. The two stood posted at a bar. It played pretty well. The rumbling ceased, mostly.

Then Kool G. Rap entered the video frame.

"What the fuck!" shouted Tupac.

And everybody began to beat the shit out of Sam Sneed. Fists, legs, whatever. Everybody at that meeting got a lick or a kick all up in his ass. I can almost see where they were coming from. Like, how are you gonna be on the Death Row team when you're hangin' out with Dre and a lot of niggas from the East?

Suge made Sneed put in an appearance at a party for Snoop that night. He even gave a toast. Then he flew home to Pittsburgh. Sam was never the same. Death Row never released the album. Not too long ago the nigga had brain surgery, just to get his ass back to some semblance of normality. The crazy shit is that Sam Sneed is my dog, but he's never owned up to exactly what happened that day at Can-Am, even though I know the deal from folks that was there. My guess is that it's hard to talk to me about it, considering I told his dumb ass not to go.

Beyond just the viciousness of Suge's shit, what bugged me about the ringleader of Death Row was his total lack of regard for the sanctity of artists and the studio. The studio is all but sacred. You can't be whuppin' niggas' asses in there and then expect hot performances to come out of that bitch tomorrow.

Chapter Thirteen

Vivian

At the height of all the insanity, I linked up big-time with a girl of my own, not at all the type of woman I had come to expect in Hollywood. It had been my habit just to fuck a gang of hot bitches, in a rotation. Vivian, however, was in a totally different league. Fuck a rotation. I wasn't even convinced that I could get with her.

We first met back in 1995, at one of the countless Dre parties. We were still doing those intimate get-togethers that felt like heaven to a cool person in Hollywood. No gawkers, not too much business. No blow. Around these times, cute little Vivian and I started to chop it up with each other. Nothing big, it was just me talking to a hot chick who just seemed like cool people. She wouldn't hang out long, but she always sought me out to say hi. She didn't want anything.

That blew me away like a breath of fresh air. You know? There are a lotta ambitious airheads in Hollywood. Dumb-ass bitches who want only cars and clothes. Beautiful as a lot of these women were physically, most of them were disappointing on the inside. (A gangsta nigga's trick is letting a girl know that we aren't as bad as we *seem*.) So when Vivian would step onto the floor with her crew—some classmates from up at San Luis Obispo, some of them girls who worked at labels and were featured in videos—I was like: Oh. What is she even *doing* here?

Vivian had an easy way about her, which I'd come to know by our third or fourth chat. Even though she had a college education, she could get her hands dirty. An athlete by nature, she was tough. Vivian had grown up knocking down walls as part of her family's home rehabilitation business. Learning these details just cinched it all. I was feeling Vivian before. A shapely black and Filipino chick? It would take a Nazi to not be feeling her. But once I got to know Vivian's background I started looking at her differently. With respect.

As the nine-nickel slipped into nine-six, I noticed that Viv never went home with anyone. She would just get in early and party with her friends. Always dancing with her friends. And sometimes with herself. She always came up in the spot looking good and together. Not one time did she make a drunken fool of herself. And she ain't fuck no niggas!

At least no one who would talk about it. And these niggas would talk about it.

"I need a girl like Vivian," observed more than one member of the Death Row fam.

So, I copped her number, finally, and gave Viv a holler. We talked on the phone a *bunch*. I learned she had a boyfriend, sorta. But she wasn't really feeling him, and that was dope. We were feeling each other. I'd been around a lot of girls, though, and it was kinda cool how this one affected me. Vivian wasn't as much into gangsta music, and neither was I. Not all the time. We found out that there was a lot more to each other than how we portrayed ourselves.

Can you imagine? Me, the guy who started out ballin' in this town with Robin and her freaky friends and then *really* started doin' the nasty, wanted to compromise and settle down. I wanted Vivian. Resting became impossible until I could convince her to be my girlfriend. Comes a time you don't want to get left standing in the cold. Maybe Dre's slowing down with Nicole was an influence.

I was eight years older than Vivian, but that was not the issue. It was the Death Row shit. As if the increasing party edge—a beatdown here, gunshots there—wasn't making clear what my work life was like, all she had to do was watch the news. We were on the local news all the time, and not for Good Samaritan of the Week. Vivian just couldn't get past my label affiliation. She wasn't supposed to be messin' with some Death Row dude. A turning point was the admission to myself that the gangsta nonsense was getting to me as well.

The Suge scene was intriguing to her at first. It was supposed to be a party thrill, not the place you'd meet a serious boyfriend. What would her parents say? They paid a lot of that college tab. I got that. But Death Row was a part of what I did for a living. It was not essential to who I was. Parts of me just didn't fit into Death Row. I thought we should just be making records.

The things that took me and Dre to Aftermath were the things that got us with our women.

C'mon now: The Snoop trial. Tupac and this cop. Tupac at that club. Suge. I had been down with these niggas as a lieutenant for Dre. At the end of the day, though, I just wasn't that far out. My ass was in the military. I wasn't just some thug nigga. The job description for me was helping out my man. The girl and her parents needed to understand that.

So one Friday afternoon I drove out to her apartment in the San Fernando Valley. Vivian and I were gonna sort this thing out for real. Either she was going to be with me or not. I might not have been the hardest G in Los Angeles, but I was not trying to get punked by some relationship.

As I wove through North Hollywood to Vivian's apartment, a familiar figure came into view. I'd only heard him described. He was out front, near her car, and I knew instantly that he was the competition.

Mayn, fuck that nigga. With my windows down, I phoned Vivian and told her to come on down. And here he comes with a tough expression across his face.

"Whassup," he said. "Who you here to see?'

"What's it to you, nigga?"

"Who you here to see?"

"Vivian," I said. "So? What's up?"

"You a Nupe?" he asked.

"A 'Nupe'? What the fuck is a 'Nupe'? I ain't no motherfuckin' *Nupe*."

That sounded like gangsta to me. Nupe. And I definitely was not trying to get involved with some odd shit. I didn't know what a Nupe was. I just knew that I wasn't one.

I got on the phone with Vivian again and told her what was going on. Was I gonna have to knock this man out? I told her I was gonna have to hit her up later. Peace out.

That night I drove back east, arriving in Palm Springs at about 1 A.M. As soon as I could grab a phone, I called Vivian. She made me be quiet and listen. "Nupe" was slang for a member of the Kappa Alpha Psi fraternity. That guy was asking if I was a Kappa. If I had known the word it would have been fine. Since I didn't, there was static. He wasn't going to let me just pick up on his girl, no matter what.

But Vivian told me she wanted to be with me. She wasn't thinking about that frat boy.

Man, I was so happy I told her to get out there that night. Vivian caught the next plane out to the desert and next thing you know she was at the kitchen table talking to my mom.

She would tell me that I'm a good listener, no matter how confrontational I could make a mode. Having a woman of my girl's caliber notice me the way she did really affected me. Viv would take me by the shoulders and slow me down when I got too busy to state my needs. She taught me how to ask for things. Emotional things.

And I just loved her like family. I kidded Vivian that she was just like Dre, another flaky Sagittarius.

Beef was cookin' so tough in those days of label transition, I told certain friends like Lakers guard Nick Van Exel that we couldn't hang

out for a while. I was just thinking about their safety. Relatively inno-
cent bystanders like Big Jake were catching fatal bullets.

Yet the Death Row era's end came to pass without me getting
touched at all. One near-miss told me just how much relationships
suffered in this battle for money and power and control over Dre.

It was at Benihana. I was with Vivian when I ran into the singer
Michel'le. She didn't know Vivian at the time. Nobody knew my
brand-new girl. She just didn't get down that way. Anyway, Michel'le
was at the bar and had all these carry-out bags. I had always liked
her. We talked all the time, about damn near everything. And the
truth is, I missed her as much as I did anyone who was no longer
rolling with us. I thought that, if I hurried, I could catch her before
she split.

"Michel'le! I haven't seen you in a really long time," I told her. It occurred to me that I should introduce Vivian. "This is my girl Viv.
What's goin' on?"

Dre's ex made time with us. Just shootin' the shit, because we were
cool like that.

After nearly ten minutes, Vivian and I go on, do what we've got to
do. Getting to the table takes a little while. The restaurant was pretty
crowded. And it's Benihana, so you know that they've got to chop
everything up and put on the little show. It takes some time to eat our
meal.

Right around the time the check's about to come, I look up and I
see Suge's best friend, Buntry, and another cat I know by face, not
name.

Yep, I'm thinkin', it's about to go down. I told Viv to go wait in
the car.

They bogart a table next to me while I'm waiting to pay the tab.
White people are lookin' at us all crazy.

I left my money, grabbed my doggy bags, walked by their table, and
said, "Whassup, mayn?"

"Say, mayn," Buntry starts. "You know that Range Rover? We need the keys by twelve noon tomorrow. And we need a hundred Gs for pullin' security."

"A hundred Gs? Didn't y'all get paid for that by Death Row?"

They had been paid already, no question. Suge's boy? That was the first cat who was getting a check. And it wasn't even credible that Dre would be responsible for that particular expense.

"Naw. And we need the keys to the truck. The homey Suge bought that."

"Shit, Suge ain't bought that. I took the paperwork over to the dealership my damn self. We're still paying notes on that. What are you talking about?"

"Well, we need the keys."

"Let me get this straight," I said. If he could feel my sarcasm, I was gonna be hella happy. "You need the keys to the Range Rover that Suge never bought. A hundred Gs for security y'all already got paid for. And you need it by tomorrow at twelve. That's it? Anything else? Y'all good?"

"Yeah, yeah. We good."

So, that went pretty well, I thought. They wouldn't do anything in the restaurant, but it was natural that they'd try to follow me. The route to where I'd parked at the Ventura Boulevard Benihana called for a walk along the alley, so I kept my back to the wall.

I spotted Vivian at the car, and she looked as though she were exhaling after holding a very long breath. To be honest, it felt pretty good to me, too, that we looked to be getting out of there without any bullshit jumping off.

But then I looked off to the opening of the parking lot and who did I see driving off, but Michel'le—damn near two hours after I'd talked to her!

Wait. Could it really have been my *friend* Michel'le who called Suge's goons? That hurt. It's like you tell yourself not to think your relationships aren't all business when really they are. I mean, think about it: she had waited around. What the hell was she trying to do? Or, more accurately, what was she trying to see? I know Michel'le had been hung up over Dre—especially because his wife, Nicole, isn't black—but never would I have believed this girl would set me up. But why? I had no idea what she was trying to do.

Chapter Fourteen

G'd Up Enough

Hard core West Coast hip hop changed me. Around this time, one of my friends from back home came to visit me in L.A. He couldn't help but be around my work. Back then my pager was goin' off, like, all the fucking time. And I'd scream on niggas, straight blow their hair back. On the phone or in person, if you had a job to do and didn't come through for me, I was letting niggas have it with both barrels. It didn't matter who you were. Captain Curseout was in fine form.

"What *happened* to you?" he said, with absolute mystery in his eyes.

That was my gig, the hard guy. I was the one who cut no slack because someone needed to keep this hip-hop thing together.

A part of it was confidence. All the things around rap music are designed to make you or break you. There's some proving ground in MCing, but the thing is different from what's with the military. Both the Louisiana prison and the Army showed me how to really push myself mentally and physically, but there's something spiritual about hip hop. It's in the music.

All the purist hip-hop historical types always like to talk about the four elements of hip hop: MCing, DJing, b-boying and graf writing, but they say the elements like they're always on an equal par. At first the rappers were at the top of the food chain. If any niggas was making any real money, and most weren't, it was the rappers. Death Row brought that out more than anybody. You'll never again see a rapper as hot as Tupac was at the end of his life. And did you ever really see a DJ in a Death Row video?

The DJ was Dre, pulling strings from the back, on some art for art's sake level. While all the other rap names were stocking their portfolios with pop acts and brand-name goods to sell, he kept ownership of gangsta rap. When he left Death Row, Suge just got the name, for whatever that would turn out to be worth. Because Death Row was always about Dr. Dre's sound.

How could I not change, just bein' around Dre's vibe? It took confidence to prank the whole biz and steer it his way. The whole culture, actually. Transforming that. And the confidence developed at an individual level. Like, watching Snoop blossom as an artist, just turn into one of the all-time greats, has been something of a blessing for me. Mostly it's just educational. Watching this shy C-walkin' stoner start in the game out of sheer love. Snoop was straight out of the group 213 when "Deep Cover" hit. He wasn't ready for the rocket ride. Yet, he stayed with it, strengthened his national posture by linking up with Master P, and let everything he went through work as a lesson.

I don't have to get Warren G and Nate Dogg to tell you that what Snoop sold me and the world was a distinctively L.A. gangsta kind of confidence. The chronic of confidence. And my out-of-town friend just wasn't hip to the dynamic. Screaming had to happen with some people, I told him. You just caught me on a day when I got a bunch of idiots.

And Los Angeles can sometimes seem filled with airheads and idiots. So, you really need to get rough with folks to set things straight.

Gangsta.

I don't know if it's right, but I know that it's true.

You might think it was all hunky-dory, escaping from the everyday Blood rawness to form Aftermath but you would be wrong. The game was still dirty at Interscope, only the beatdowns took place in board-rooms rather than alleys. By the late 1990s, when crack was turned back—its heyday having come during the Reagan era—corporate America beat the streets for the title of Shadiest Enclave in the U.S. of A. In 1999, the music biz would consolidate, giving even more clout to the few giant labels. Companies selling all sorts of products would begin openly beating a path to doors of raw street artists, instead of doing it on the sly as they had in the past. In terms of gangsta music, the end of the twentieth century was a corporate clusterfuck.

So, in some ways moving to Aftermath was out of the frying pan and into the fire. Just replace a nigga's hair grease with some Brylcreem and you'll know exactly what's up.

Look at the top of the music industry, at the old, rich white dudes who own record companies. How much do they spend on artist development? Zilch. That says everything. If you're not gonna spend anything on nurturing the artists you're trying to sell, then how do you expect to keep sellin'?

I tend to focus all of my criticisms on Jimmy Iovine, but he's far from an idiot. He's just a cynic, a guy so defined by the idea that business isn't personal that he'll just fuck cats over because that's how the old school told him to do it. Dude was like my old military seniors, not the brass but the ones who went out of the way to be assholes. Short guys, a lot of them.

Anyway, the rap music biz didn't just get fucked up yesterday. Jimmy's from back in the day *before* yesterday, and the blame can't even be placed squarely at his feet. Blame belongs to a time before there was hip hop on records. It started back in the day. When Barry White was on CBS Records, you didn't have release dates. Them cats put out dope records when they felt they had dope records. But this was when the movie part of CBS wasn't paying attention to what the music division was doing.

Then one day someone in management looked at the overall books and figured the record business was worth $2 billion. And they moved bean counters—accountants, lawyers—over to the music side. These hacks are the ones who invented the idea that one artist had to release an album this quarter and the other had to release one the next quarter. It's been downhill ever since. Time constraints, rigid budgets—however inflated or undervalued—and other bottom-line thinking poisoned creativity.

That came during disco, somewhere in the 1970s between Sly Stone exiting the scene and Teddy Pendergrass going solo. Only now, in the face of technological challenges and a lot of financial players at the labels, does the game look really fucked up, but it's been ailing for a while. Like a patient who *appears* okay, but inside is riddled with disease. At the worst of times, the biz looks sick like Eazy looked sick.

These days, just about nobody left in the business has nuts. Only every once in a while will you see someone try something new. A&R reps don't know what they're doin'. They don't know what's goin' on and they're telling artists how to do their album. And the sad truth is that they're tryin' to get the artist to do another cat's hit. No nuts.

Now, here I am not talking about Jimmy Iovine. That guy's nuts? Ginormous. He's *gangsta*. Jimmy was supremely positioned to run a record label. He knew how it would make sense in the long haul to comfort Dre instead of scare him. Where Suge ran things on some ol' Don King, y'all my serfs type-shit, Jimmy truly valued Dre, if *only* as a moneymaker.

He wanted a big act. *Aftermath Presents* had been a big introduction. The label was at a crucial point in its brief history through 1997. The idea had been for the company to release a second Dre solo album. But the rapper-producer didn't have *The Chronic* franchise installment ready. Jimmy said it was cool, he didn't want to wreck the brand. That was the franchise.

And then he went out to something called The Rap Olympics, and that night he saw a fierce MC battle. When he got hip hop fully, it really excited him. He'd base *8 Mile* on it one day. Very deep. Primal.

Rock 'n' roll. And this black chick freestyled all over her opponent, who gave her a really tough time right back. Line for line, seminal L.A. underground hip hop.

But it wasn't the winner he wanted. She was old, at least thirty. A thirty-year-old black chick with an Afro and an attitude? He didn't see it, no matter how talented the woman was.

But the runner-up. A white kid. Not too tall and real intense. Blue eyes, brunette, and not too remarkable-looking. Maybe they could bleach his hair or something. Jimmy congratulated the kid, said he should have won and hit him up for a demo. The kid who had dreamed for years of being signed to Death Row had no idea to whom he was talking.

One of Jimmy's runners got a tape of the dude. The runner passed it on to the exec, who put it in a pile and forgot about the thing. This tape made its way to Jimmy's garage. One day Dre came across it while shooting the shit with his boss.

"What's that?"

Jimmy said that he didn't know. Dre played it and was knocked the fuck out. The two looked at each other.

"Find that cat!"

Jimmy's people worked overtime to track down the artist's Detroit number. Then Dre called up Marshall Mathers and offered a free plane ticket to Los Angeles. I set up the meeting. From then on it was simple. We put him in the studio days later and Aftermath had its first new star. His first recordings were exactly what the company needed.

I shouldn't have even been caring about big issues such as the direction of music. What was it to me, the man *next to* the man—a dude who was feeling a little removed from the process since After-math's earliest days? At the end of the day I was the guy who made sure all the chairs were set up at the start of an event. Now I'd become an antiseptic version of the guy who had earlier made sure no bullshit was goin' down at night's end, who made sure that nothing was stolen or broken. We had interns and whatnot to do that shit now. Still, my career just wasn't evolving the way I felt it should. Despite all the famous friends and a very flossy datebook, I still kissed my girl good-bye each day and went off to the job of making other people happy at my own expense.

It's contradictory in some ways because the crew we rolled with now was less street, but just as entertaining as the people at Death Row. Mel-Man was the most interesting. For example, he didn't drink. He didn't need to; the guy was buck-wild stone sober. Then we took him to a Puerto Rican restaurant in Manhattan's Soho neighborhood and convinced him to drink a Long Island Iced Tea. He fell asleep, head smack-dab atop the table—regardless of all the approachable, fine bitches in our presence. After that, Mel-Man turned into one of the harder drinkers running among us. And we did indeed party. It was like we were on alert for a party to break out. If somebody said "party in ten minutes," you best believe that we got it crackin'. That's something I admired about the Aftermath staff, even at the worst of times.

Individually, you couldn't knock them. This was the new family; with new cats like J-Boogie, Mike Lynn and Philip Atwell in the mix, a new crew was beginning to take shape. And if fam weren't the hub of it all I'd have called in sick a lot more.

The fun became a lot more mature. Like, we had an ongoing competition to see who could cook the best turkey tacos. So now the barbecues focused a lot less on topless girls in swimming pools—oh, the girls were still there, but things were a lot more low-key—and more on cook-offs for the title of Barbecue King. Of course, I was the best. But, for real? If you asked every one of us—Dre, Mike Lynn, it doesn't matter—we'd each say we were the greatest.

Don't get it twisted: Suge wasn't the only cat at our old label that was sometimes on some bullshit. My friend would orchestrate drama, then sit back and watch the show. Aftermath's newfangled workplace brand of shit-talking could still make the idea of getting up and going to work at a high-profile, outwardly alluring gig absolutely not sexy. Quickly, the crew fell into backbiting and gossip. I admit it, there would be drama because I wasn't feeling Mike Lynn. (His only function seemed to be doing exactly what Jimmy asked. If I wanted to be around yes-men, I figured, a career in the military would have been my route.) Or maybe it was that J-Boogie had called Philip Atwell a square one time too many. The crew was the crew, a collection of personalities. The way we co-existed couldn't help but take a toll on me.

This time was hella bizarre. I was breathing easier because the air of physical threat was gone. It seemed like the perfect time to solidify our team and get all the projects—the film and TV proposals—in place. We were going to actualize our collected talent, I thought. Instead, everyone pursued individual agendas and we all became wage slaves on the record plantation. That includes well-paid slaves like Dre. However, Aftermath was also having less allure because I was getting so into Vivian. Here was a woman who understood what a hard time my job had become. From the outside, everything must have seemed lovely. No question work was more comfortable now at Aftermath. (The effect of guns in the workplace kinda creeps up on you, but once guns finally stop being around on the daily, you get a real lift. Every piece of weaponry you see after that takes on a shine of its own.) No doubt the times were exciting. But Vivian was the only person outside my relationship with Dre who saw why I stuck around. Dre was the brother I never had, an upgrade even from my uncles and half brothers who are very dear to me. If he was going through that shit, I was going through that shit. And in Viv I finally had someone who could maybe go through it with me.

Vivian was pursuing a business degree at California Polytechnic State University while also working a small-time job low on the Aftermath food chain. One night, just before she left the company, Dre took me aside in the studio. It was late and I thought he wanted to talk about a music-related issue.

"Man, don't let that one get away," he said. "I know you run through all these women, but there doesn't seem to be one that tickles your fancy. You fuck things up with Vivian, and I'll kick your ass my damn self!"

It was dope to hear Dre say this. It only reinforced my sense of him as the big brother I never had. But I did recognize what I had in this woman.

I felt like we would do big things.

My dreams had included owning a building. I had wanted one of those big downtown skyscrapers since I started driving in from Palm Springs for acting lessons.

That dream was realized a little when Vivian started talking about running a nightclub. She was tired of waiting in line at nightspots, and the rest of us in Dre's crew were looking for a place to chill. It was early in the Aftermath history—we may have still been calling the label Black Market—but we were still Dr. Dre and his boys. Going out for us meant being besieged with industry favors when all we wanted was to relax.

Vivian located a place she thought was perfect. It seemed homey to her. But the club, Vertigo, was located downtown near Sunset and Temple. I was not fucking with downtown Los Angeles. In 1997, no one I knew was fucking with downtown L.A. But I supported my girl despite my reservations.

"Damn, Viv, will they come?" I asked her.

"They'll come! They'll come." She said she had noticed small improvements happening downtown.

I don't know if Vivian was sure but her ass sure was right. They came.

Not so much at first. Actually, the crowd wasn't that thick in the opening weeks. Mostly the parking lot and dance floor were populated by our circle of Interscope people. Then on the third Friday, the place, which on Friday nights we called Creep Alley, just filled up. Packed with a full lot and long line early in the evening.

The women who showed up were stupid fine. I had to get on the phone with the fellas back at the studio. "Man, you need to get up off that bullshit and come down to the club. Nothin' but women in here!"

It wasn't an advertised spot and business built up by word of mouth. Years before the Las Vegas campaign, we handed out cards stating that "What happens at Creep Alley stays there." A selective cut of young, hip Hollywood just started showing up. Even Lisa Kudrow from the show *Friends* strolled her skinny self up in there.

Creep Alley had two rooms, each with its own DJ who would compete with each other to see who could keep their room hotter. Shaq would be in the crowd. Tichina Arnold who was then on *Martin.* The Wayanses. They all would be partying their asses off. And if it got too hot you could always step out onto the patio, and if you were so inclined, smoke yourself a J.

We stayed open until 4 A.M. and then unsigned, unknown artists such as DMX and Eve would step to the stage, for free, and rock the mic. Our vibe was like a jam session. Mike Lynn kept the night going by playing the hypeman role. He'd step to the mic and yell, "On the count of three, everybody freeze! One . . . Two . . . Freeze!"

The crew and I would be laughing and saying, "Mike, you doin' the stupidest shit!"

But them niggas did freeze, and Creep Alley was indeed hot as an oven.

After about a year, Vivian and I decided to break the platinum cards for good and call it quits. The whole club experience was exhausting. All week long I was supplementing my Aftermath work with my Creep Alley work. Friday was basically all about the club. And since the spot stayed open until 4 A.M., I wasn't getting home until about seven in the morning. Saturday was shot. Doing Creep Alley burned me out.

But to be honest, I really hated being around all those gorgeous, sexually liberated women late at night. My guys would constantly be pointing out the finest and I wanted to play but I couldn't. I was with my old lady.

The main thing was that we weren't making enough money. It was fun and all, but Creep Alley left us just slightly better off than we were before the club.

It wasn't the big thing Vivian and I were meant to do.

We got married in the spring of 1998, at The Lighthouse in Pacific Palisades. 1998. My new wife was twenty-six, but struck me as just so grown. She was just seriously starting to give thought to the real estate game—another legacy of her father. I really liked Vivian's family, both her black daddy and her Filipino mommy. Baby's family from all over the state was at our wedding. Them and my people and her friends made about one hundred in all. It seemed like a good fit. And if they did think of me then as a young hothead, that was understood. They treated me like a nice guy.

When it came to my marriage, I couldn't complain. Vivian didn't question everything I did. If I didn't come home until early in the morning—and that happened a lot, as hip hop doesn't really get started most times until after midnight—she wouldn't bother me about that. There's never been an issue of her calling me all the time to check and see if I'm actually at the studio. None of that.

What single people don't understand is that it's about a respect level and a trust thing whenever you really get with somebody. It's how you carry yourself. If I thought she'd come into contact with another girl that I was to even *think* about messin' with, I would never mess with that girl. Girls always know if you're fuckin' around. There's something about them that allows girls to know. So I never wanted to do something like that, and I never wanted them to cross paths.

That's why a lot of girls just thought I was an asshole. But it wasn't like that. It was more like:

Trick, I know you talk too fuckin' much. You know my inner circle and you talkin' on my fellas, so what the fuck? You think *I'm* gonna fuck with you? My niggas can deal with that shit. If I married Vivian, I must have put her up on a pedestal. So why would I put this trick-ass bitch that I might fuck with up on the same pedestal as her?

With her watching me in the business, she knew who I was. She knew I wasn't no cat out there tryin' to fuck everything shakin' and movin'—not to say that she didn't think I didn't fuck *nothin'* either, now; she'd say, "If anybody's gonna fuck I'd say it's you."

I'd go out of town and she wouldn't even know what hotel I was in. If she knew the hotel, she didn't know the room number; she'd just call on the cell phone if she called at all. I went anywhere I wanted.

Actually, that was her thing. It got to the point back in the day where I wasn't tryin' to be around the Aftermath staff just because I didn't need all that extra drama—we were about to have Sir, our first son.

"Bruce," she said, "why don't you just go hang out?"

And I was like, "Eh. I'm just not feeling it right now."

In this business, if so-called sexual fidelity is what you're gonna worry about in a relationship or a marriage then you shouldn't even get together in the first place. When you got married, you said those words: through sickness and health. Everybody figures when you get married it's gonna be hunky-dory. But we're still just people.

If you're worrying about trust, you're missing out on life. In marriage a couple just has to work through things. So, where Viv was concerned, I couldn't complain. I couldn't even front.

Whatever patience I had for my work situation came from what I had at home. In Vivian, I had the kind of understanding woman who could empathize even with Dre. She suggested to me that he was moving through the world with less urgency because of his stable home life and place in Interscope's hierarchy.

Dre would always say that he preferred to get a less talented artist with a lot of hustle than a talented artist with no hustle. In Marshall Mathers he got the rare combination of talent and hustle. This white boy was *hungry.* Plus, there's probably never been a hip-hop lyricist as powerful as he was at the start of his career.

Eminem's first song was "Hi, My Name Is." Because the hip-hop world is all black, he really did face a form of racism; nobody wanted to sign a white rapper. Too many had failed in the past, and to a lot of labels and critics and fans it just looked like a gimmick when a white kid even graced record store shelves. No one wanted to risk credibility.

But Eminem won MC battles all the time, even the One Hundred MCs Battle, a massive L.A. contest in 1997. He came out from Detroit, rode around L.A. with the Bass Brothers and his lawyer/manager Paul Rosenberg, a former rapper, and worked twice as hard as everybody else, yet still remained unsigned. A less talented black kid could get a deal before him. Luckily Dre got ahold of Em's tape before he disappeared into the trailer parks of Detroit for good.

Em was in love with Kim, his baby's mama, and had a lot of problems, but he was smart. He would take pills and chase it with Hen Dog while working on his record. His writing style was off the hook with the hate and anger he grew up with. The pills and Hen Dog made him able to cope with the world and write the sickest shit. He was like a tornado in the studio. Dre struggled to commit the best of it to digital tape.

In time Eminem proved he could write bomb songs without getting high, but in the beginning it fueled his motivation. And Dre would piece his raps in, line by line—same as with neophyte rapper Eazy-E—so that every word came through with clarity. And Em went with it, ego be damned. He might say a single line twenty-five times, just to give his producer the proper effect and absolute clarity. This kid was gonna let the world know about so-called white-trash folks' lives.

When Em came onboard with his skills, Dre was back into doing what he did best: making music. That spark caught fire and it was time to let the world know that he was *still* the shit. More important, it was crucial to making Aftermath a household name. We were hanging out with people like Warren Beatty, easily the most impressive person I met in my travels through Los Angeles and beyond, and Oliver Stone, doin' big thangs. Dre and his assistant, Mel-Man, went to work, bringing in a young production gun with no name recognition by the name of Scott Storch, another Caucasian star Dre helped to launch. That's how *The Chronic 2001* began to take shape.

We had always used Reno a lot to relax. With *The Chronic 2001,* Dr. Dre's second solo project, it became an incubator for his art. In Los Angeles, there were obligations—personal and professional—at every turn. We could shut ourselves up in a studio, but outstanding checks and girlfriend crap and artists looking for their shots made their way into our world. The studio hadn't really been sacred since *Doggystyle,* if you think about it.

In Nevada the whole vibe was different. Reno was a safe haven where we could just go create. Hardly anybody recognized us if we indeed went out. And, unless we were out grubbin', the crew hardly deviated from the path between our hotel and the old house that was home to our studio. We'd roll to the gym for a workout and hardly ever gambled. We moved through town with only music on our mind. And I bet ya no one who saw the half dozen or so of us piling into one van ever guessed we were toiling away on one of the most anticipated albums of the decade.

There was still another Bruce, Big Bruce, the bodyguard. We hadn't really screwed around with having steady security until all the ugliness at the end of Death Row came down. Both Jimmy and Dre's mother insisted that he get regular protection. At 6' 7", Big Bruce was definitely that. He was also a character.

One evening in the basement of the old house we used as our studio, Big Bruce arrived early, when only the engineer and a couple of other people were there, making sure everything was set. No artists were around. Dre was off doing some preproduction business in another part of the house.

"I wanna go to the movies," he announced to Big Larry, the project coordinator.

Big Larry laughed him off, thinking, "How's he going to the movies when we're committed to being in the studio?"

"Larry, wanna go to the movies?"

"I can't go to the movies, man! I'm workin'!"

When Dre came into the studio, he found a Post-it note on the door.

"Gone to the movies. If you need me, call."

That just got bigger and funnier as the day went on and eventually erupted into everybody fuckin' with Dre. I was kiddin' him like, "If some shit *does* break out, just tell them muthafuckas to hold up. Can't nothin' go down until Bruce gets back. He's at the movies. Tell the killers he'll be right back!" Dre was like, "Fuck you. Fuck all y'all."

But every ten seconds someone would tease:

"Security!"

And then:

"Oh, wait. We ain't got no security. Hold up with the guns, mayn! Our security's at the movies. Let's have a do-over when he gets back."

We had the worst luck with security cats. One guy called me in the morning and said he was gonna miss work that day. Turns out, he had shot and killed his wife and had just turned himself in. Around the studio we were all like, "Muthafucka, whatchu mean you gon' miss a day? Nigga, you ain't *never* comin' back in to work. Be real!"

Once I got called home from Reno and there was nothing funny about it at all. Dre's mom, Verna, was on the phone. She called to tell me that the police wanted to talk to me about the murder of Christopher Wallace, aka Notorious B.I.G. Things were always awkward between me and Sean Combs even though I never had a problem with the cat, but Big and I were friendly.

Verna sounded worried, so I flew back to town and drove to the West Valley police station out in Tarzana. An officer told me that he knew that Wallace and I were friends. I told him that Big and I could only be so tight considering where I worked.

They showed me a bunch of photos of brothas. Of course I knew a lot of them, but I didn't tell the police that.

"Don't know 'im," I said to every single image. "Hey, are you anywhere near solvin' this case? Because if you're talking to me, you have no clue what's goin' on."

How do you put together a sequel to the most influential rap album of all time?

That was the question Dre had to ask himself when he did *The Chronic* more than half a decade ago. *The Chronic* was basically the N.W.A. sequel. People sometimes forget that Cube and MC Ren helped dominate that album. Dre's a strong vocal presence, but he needs a writer to come with the words that he'll articulate so profoundly. Dr. Dre doesn't care any more about the words as much as he does the drums, so he's inclined to lean on someone, a young gun. Words are a means to a sound, an effect. He'll tell the writer exactly what he wants to talk about. He changes words and phrases once the rhyme is written. It's an easy gig for a writer, mostly because Dr. Dre has accomplished so much. For Andre Young's first solo album it was Snoop who carried the ball. And he would be richly rewarded. This time the handoff went to Eminem. He came up to Reno with an idea for "Forgot About Dre." Limited, pinch-hitter cats like Knocturnal came through to hit a few homers in the studio, too.

We had a new team in place, too. Musician Mike Elizondo was there to help get the guitars and keyboards right. Mel-Man had the fattest drum sounds in Southern California. J-Boogie helped keep the hangout vibe real cool. And I was there at the control board, sitting next to Dre.

Dre uses ghostwriters because it takes him too long to write; he'd rather focus on the music. He told Jay-Z, who wrote "Still D.R.E.," exactly what he wanted that song to be about: How he still abhors five-oh, his desire to help young black kids get paid—just how he gets down overall. Then he sent Jay the beat. And then when Jay turned it in, Dre went over the lyrics. The D.O.C., who had penned his own take, read it, too.

"Damn, look at the shit that I wrote. Great minds think alike," D.O.C. told me. His version was *that* close to Jay's version.

Dre made changes and recorded it. (The two were never in the studio together.) He added Snoop's chorus and knew immediately that the crucial smash first single was in hand.

Coming in as it did behind Eminem's still-hot record, *The Chronic 2001* went mainstream fast, way faster than the first solo joint. The world was in a different place at this point in history. Jay-Z had made "Hard-Knock Life" and pushed street music even deeper into America's heart. The world was ready. All that pioneering shit was over. Planet Earth was safe for gangsta rap.

Xzibit came out on that album. Nate Dogg, still awaiting his proper solo joint, did his thing. Even Kokane and King T got on. And of course there was Snoop, who had just about finished rollin' with Master P and was now a truly upper-echelon MC. He brought his A-game for Dre. In all, the second *Chronic* played as homage to the West Coast underground. Instant classic. Objectively better than the first.

The real eye-opener was on tour, which Magic Johnson had hooked up. He was trying to get in on the promotion game and won the bid to handle what we called the Up in Smoke tour. Almost immediately we needed him. In Detroit, the mayor's office shut us down over a show-opening video created especially for the tour that they claimed might move the audience to violence, failing to see the artistic value of director Phil Atwell's gangsta piece. It had violent imagery of guns and other drama, but Atwell is indeed an artist.

Magic Johnson's call to help went nowhere. And he's *from* East Lansing. We had to threaten to sue. That's exactly how much opposition hip hop can generate, from black as well as white. The next night we actually got to show the film over in the white part of town. Those kids went so nuts, you could just see the police lined up around the arena hating every single minute of what they saw. But it was a great show. I only wish the black kids had been able to see the event in its intended form.

In Utah, fans petitioned to get Up in Smoke in their town. They had never had a single meaningful rap concert in Salt Lake City. And once we hit Idaho, the locals filled up a little bandbox of an arena with ridiculous heat and energy. My *clothes* vibrated from the noise. I swear to you, I've never seen an audience more into a show. They literally craved hip hop. It was so loud I couldn't hear myself think. It was hard to imagine what Dre and Snoop, Eminem and Ice Cube were feeling with all that electricity directed at them. Oh my God! There's no drug in the world that's better than the energy from fans. And you wonder why performers have a hard time walkin' away. To have thousands of people passionately yelling your name *has* to produce a feeling that can't be duplicated anywhere.

I worked out a lot with Magic Johnson, and during those times he'd say insightful stuff. It seemed to me he was holding back, though. After he began opening up to me a few years later, the entrepreneur finally did admit that he had kept his guard up in my presence.

"You weren't ready," Magic told me. "I could have told you lots of things you just weren't prepared to hear."

He was right. I was in a fog back then, just riding the wave. In my business, hanging on too long with nowhere to land could be deadly.

Times got less dangerous when Dre left Death Row. But they didn't necessarily become easier.

Sometimes we felt just a little bit too secluded. The tour ended, and there we were huddled up in the studio.

For a while I was fooling around with music myself. We had a studio inside the spot over on Pico and I'd filled a drum machine full of sounds. It was my time to take a shot at making a track.

Then, of course, Dre walks in.

"Man, let me show you how to make a motherfuckin' beat! You ain't makin' no beats."

Now, I knew it wasn't in his nature to do anything but clown a new booty such as myself, but, dayum, at least let me get started!

"Who gave you these wack-ass sounds?" Dre asked when he couldn't conjure up something immediately.

"You!" I answered quickly. "Yo' ass gave me them wack-ass beats!"

And that was the end of that.

But I did make a rap song with Bud'ah, Ice Cube's producer. It wasn't bad, but it was never something I would release. Bud'ah had me put in one of my signature expressions at the time: "Less than a damn" as in "I could give less than a damn." Dre acted as if he liked my song after he found it in a trash pile.

"You should have kept it up," he suggested. "We could have made a video and could have made it funny."

"That's all fine and dandy," I told my boss, "but I need to go run Aftermath."

We did get out a little bit. The crew went out to a Hollywood Hills house party. It was a different style from how we got down with Death Row.

Kid Rock was in the house and I'd totally forgotten he could deejay. Dre and Em started rapping over the record Kid Rock spun. We didn't do enough of that stuff, but when we did it stole the show.

We didn't do that stuff because Dre preferred hanging out with small groups. He was assured top billing and nobody would bother him for music. You might find us upstairs at a cheesy spot on Sunset like Red Rock trying out records on a natural uncynical audience— but not out there rubbing noses with our natural strata of the game.

Eminem did a lot to get Dre back on the radar. And *2001* took things to another level. It was almost as bright a scenario, product-wise, as the biggest days of Death Row. But we needed more dope artists and there were missteps. Xzibit, who had been such a presence on Dre's second solo album, looked like he was set to be a superstar. Dre loved his rap, his aggressive energy and enthusiasm. Unfortunately X, who was on Loud rather than Aftermath, fucked up his credibility by disavowing Snoop Dogg when confronted by Suge Knight. After about a decade of Dre publicly calling Rakim the one artist he wanted to work with, the legend signed with Aftermath and looked to be the guy who would put up major numbers for a long time. But Rakim was not the rapper he once was. He didn't even rhyme in the studio with the crew hanging out. Dude was writing only at home. Dre wanted to do tracks in a way that allowed you to feel the camaraderie. Rakim's a legend, but he was legend in his day. The chemistry between these two just wasn't there. Times had changed, and with a title like "Oh My God," which Rakim's album was set to be called, the material had to be way above par. There would be no Rakim album on Aftermath. A lot of his songs would go to Aftermath's next big star, a guy from Queens who would turn the industry on its ear.

King T's album never came out, either. He had some great songs, but they weren't ones that were gonna come out and really *bang*. That might sound harsh, but people have to remember that our label had to sell a gang of albums. *Aftermath Presents* sold a million fucking albums and it was considered a bust. King Tipsy is a legend. His image, though, was that of the homey on the corner in a white tee and sportin' a sawed-off shotgun. Now, for this video, he did a 180 and hit the set dressed in a suit and had girls dancin' around him. No way in the world that shit was gonna fly. Dayum!

Then, just before things got to be seriously problematic, the answer revealed himself: Curtis "50 Cent" Jackson.

50 Cent and me was always cool. A lot of rappers talk about loving to be hated. This cat literally thrives on it. Born Curtis Jackson, he was from Jamaica, Queens. Fiddy actually was a good dude, at least when he came around us. He had history as a drug dealer and was hungry because no one wanted to give him a deal. Fiddy had signed a production deal with the late, great Jam Master Jay, but that didn't go anywhere. Tha Trackmasterz, a hot production team at the time, were working with Columbia Records and offered him a deal, if he got out of the one with Jay. It cost Fiddy fifty grand to make the move, and then he got stalled at Columbia.

Out of desperation, he wrote the song "How to Rob," in which he named names in rapping about his desire to stick up every star in the biz for their jewelry. That got 50 Cent some infamy as a lot of the bigger names acknowledged his threats both onstage and on records. But dude still ain't have no deal, and no records in stores as "How to Rob" was released strictly as a promo single. It was only a matter of time before he was back in the street, hustlin'.

That's when 50 Cent got shot. He was beefin' with Ja Rule and half of NYC when he got shot nine times. Dude was easily the most famous rapper who didn't have a record out, and he pimped the injuries bigger than anybody other than Tupac did when he first got shot. Label execs were afraid of him—he talked wild in the magazines and at record-label meetings; 50 clearly wasn't faking his bad boy rep—and didn't want to take a chance.

When Em heard 50 Cent's pioneering mixtape *50 Cent Is the Future,* he gave it to Dre. The people over at Sony/Columbia, who had originally signed him, lost their nerve and let the nigga go without putting out the album he had recorded for them. The edgy buzz that would make 50 Cent a monster in the game was keeping him on the sidelines.

Early in 2002, Aftermath called a meeting at the Mondrian hotel. Dre and Eminem had touched base on the set of Em's movie *8 Mile.* Now we all needed to know if 50 was going to be able to pull this thing off on a professional level. Rappin' in the streets and making mixtapes are a lot more friendly toward wildstyle freelancing than the commercial music industry, so there were concerns. He would be coming into the so-called Aftermath Family under Em's freshly formed Shady Records and, despite how it might look to outsiders, a sophisticated structure was most definitely in place.

Just Dre, Eminem, 50, Em's manager, Paul Rosenberg, and 50's manager, Chris Lighty, were present for the conference. Our prospect was charismatic and showed the same sort of smarts that allowed him to change the mixtape game—by turning 50 Cent appearances into must-own material—and preserve his career when it looked so extremely fucked up to regular East Coast execs. Still, we needed to find out where 50's head was at. Our camp asked about his beefs across the industry and in the street. And when he got the sense that 50 would go the distance, Dre told him to just make records and let all the other shit go. He'd tell that to every young MC I knew him to work with. It's a primary reason why you hear about Aftermath all the time and Death Row hardly at all.

"Are you ready to make history?" Dr. Dre asked 50 Cent.

And he was like, *Hell yeah!*

Like successful MCs, 50 Cent was a normal guy who had just been through some shit. He had no more baggage than any other rapper. But he had the fire to rap. And that mixtape was blowin' up. Then Sony offered 50 a million dollars to come back. So we gave him a million to run with us. Fifty knew then that if he did what we told him, he was the next star—because that's what Dre did: He made stars.

Out of nowhere, rival New Yorker Ja Rule started talking shit about 50 Cent in the press. The first inclination 50 had was to fire back immediately, but he was smart, did his shit right because he wanted to put his crew, G-Unit, on the map. It's pretty obvious he made the right moves. Anyone got the numbers on those recent Ja Rule releases? *Get Rich or Die Tryin'* sold eleven million copies worldwide and became the basis for a major motion picture. Now the man's into diverse ventures like energy drinks and book publishing.

Chapter Fifteen

More Money, More Problems

Aftermath was in the black for good by 2003. Things were moving so nicely that we didn't have to sell music if we didn't want to. Take for instance the time that the producers of the movie *Bad Boys II* starring that ol' gangsta rap nemesis, Will Smith, asked us for some music. We wouldn't give them anything new, but we did license some background music for a key scene in which Smith's and Martin Lawrence's characters are making comments that are mistaken for a sexually graphic homosexual conversation. Well, we made sure the music underneath that scene was the song "Bitch Niggaz" from *The Chronic 2001* because that's what we thought of that hater, Smith. We had to get our fun where we could find it because life in the studio just wasn't what it once had been.

Way before this point, we had stopped allowing walk-in rappers— or walk-in anyone, for that matter—at studio sessions. If you weren't down with the camp, you just weren't there.

Too many motherfuckers were suin', tryin' to say we put their sounds in beats. It was ridiculous. As we once did with rappers at Death Row, we'd let these wannabe producers watch a little bit and learn what went on in a top-flight studio. If you wanted to vibe, you vibed; it was cool. Nobody was trippin' on ya. Have a good time. But then niggas started with the frivolous lawsuits. People were suing for $10,000, $20,000. And we'd have to pay them off. C'mon!

Appearances at corporate events and rich kids' parties is something 50 and Em did to (handsomely) supplement their CD proceeds, which are a rip-off to artists anyway. Do a party and the percentage the work actually brings your way is far higher than from recorded music sales.

It's hip hop that had all athletes and fashion people and broadcasters tryin' to be fly and talk hip. And if you wanted to sell something to young people, who did companies call? The hip-hop guys. Nike. Sprite. Chrysler. At first, companies like Nike just wanted to pay sports guys and compensate hip-hop artists in clothes and whatnot. And niggas was like, *Fuck that*. We know how little it costs to manufacture that shit.

Then the rappers and them got hip to their real clout—look what Run-DMC did for Adidas and what LL Cool J did for FUBU—and started asking for real dough. Cross Colours and Karl Kani showed the mainstream how to get down with us and maximize their investment. After that it was easy for big stars to cash in. The Aftermath crew stayed mad at Dre because he cashed in on so little of this stuff. I mean, beyond that Coors Light ad he did a few years ago, how many commercials of his can you name?

It didn't take long before the labels learned to use corporate dollars as a way of offsetting their costs and get major cross-promotion, which watered down the music. And they insisted that songs with connections to their products not contain natural street lingo, especially language related to drugs or guns—regardless of context. They got all caught up in the moneymaking potential of putting just two good songs on an album and basically treating the rest of a buyer's $16.98 investment as filler. And probably most harmful of all was the way the big commercial investors embraced "bling" all out of proportion. What was once just a small aspect of the culture got projected into being its most important thing.

I couldn't help but think about the negatives of corporate influence as I watched Dr. Dre pick up the piano. Just hanging out—around the crib and in the studio—he fooled around with it and seemed to me to be naturally gifted. The next logical step, in his mind, was to go formal. You know? Figure out what he wasn't yet hearing in the music. He got that idea from working with Mel-Man, who as a producer was way above average at making slammin' drum patterns and not all that great at the other parts of making songs. They wanted to get properly educated in order to take their music to a higher level. The idea was to begin reading music and study theory. Pure artists are always looking to improve at their craft.

Mel-Man dropped out. He had a lot of shit goin' on. But Dre stayed with it. A musician by the name of Steve Lindsay would come out to the house each week and work with him at the keyboard. Before, when he would add instrumentation to a piece by re-creating samples, a lot of guesswork was at play. And please believe that back in the Death Row days there were some ill-conceived instrumentations that actually went out for public consumption. Now Dre was more precise. He became a decent piano player and more than adept at reading sheet music. The broader range of music, way beyond the standard rap arrangements, revealed themselves. This changed Doctor Dre (his name was inspired by Dr. J, another artist in a realm where artistry doesn't get its propers) in that he finally began to see permanence in his sonic creations. He started talking about his music as something young people might study in colleges. The way Tupac was starting to get taught in certain universities played into this. I'm sure his new Seattle girl had something to do with it, too. Whatever, though, he was trying to take rap music to a higher level, the level where it's just music.

Dre has said that words don't especially matter to him, that they're just another part of the music. Of the sound. Like I always say, we don't know exactly what them jazz cats are thinking or how their feelings would translate into words when we listen to their classic sides, but with rap music you do. And since it's the specific amped-up emotion of the rawest niggas, the words could sometimes get ugly and were always at least a little base. And somebody's got to take responsibility for that.

Critics would always ask why Dre never did truly progressive hip hop like Kanye West, and I'd have to say that he did. And he was the first to do it. And that was Eminem. Eminem broadened the scope of what hip hop could be on so many levels. Self-effacing. Drug-addled. Caucasian. That he was white made some people fail to see the connection, but really this was just Dre being progressive like Eazy-E was being progressive when he reached out to East Los Angeles and then to the Midwest, single-handedly making the potential for commercial hip hop something more than just a NYC/South Central/Bey Area thing. Eminem is the end of the form, in a way. Everything after that is like an exercise. He's just that great a lyricist. Some might come around who's more musical in voice than him, but you know, I have a hard time imagining a new, more radical lyricist than him at his peak of, say, 1999.

To me, Dre making the effort to do music that's not just the same old copycat shit even though he's the leader in his field is justification for any kind of collateral damage gangsta music might do to its fans, practitioners, and sellers. Everybody gets fucked, but everybody doesn't have to get fucked to *death*.

It's complicated shit. Way too complex for the corporate rap game. Jimmy wouldn't get a clue that his prize bull wanted to better himself, to be something more than big dollars to his label. That's because with Jimmy and Suge, as with any of these multinational motherfuckers out there—an exception in the first part of this century might be Clive Davis, who actually did develop Alicia Keys—we're just dollars. Just a bunch of niggers, if you wanna be real about it.

Sometimes the Aftermath team got lulled into thinking we were untouchable. It was a digital age and we were on top.

The fact that we could be actually, tangibly touched was hit home hardest when Dre got punched in the face as he walked up to receive his *Vibe* Legend Award by an unfortunate cat who had just served a long stretch in prison. Dude's family needed money, so he decided to take cash to publicly embarrass Dre. More than halfway into the show, the ex-con Jimmy Johnson approached Dre—who was standing near the stage with Nicole—and asked for an autograph. When Dre prepared to sign, Johnson punched him in the face. Quincy Jones and Snoop were onstage, preparing to give Doc the award, but Dre's bodyguards jumped on the attacker and a melee ensued.

"I can't believe this," Jones exclaimed, "Y'all messed up my rap!"

Young Buck, an Aftermath artist and G-Unit soldier, stabbed the guy and then scooted out of the building. Dre was alright, but it was a black eye for rap music and hip hop in general. I wasn't there, but got a call about it as soon as it happened. More than anything, I was stunned at the security breach. Something like that would never happen at the mainstream music awards, even though the so-called dangerous rap artists have been showing up at these events for more than a decade.

I've heard that our old Death Row rival was behind that episode. I don't know, but it was way past too bad. At least, it was very disrespectful to Quincy Jones, a guy who's done a lot for hip hop and for pop music. And if Suge was behind the attack, as so many have theorized, it was just one more thing to think about in his slow slide to irrelevance. It was as if he were trying to bring back the glory days of his shinin' at *The Source* Awards, only this time making his threats undeniably real.

At the start of Eminem's career, Dre said he would be bigger than Michael Jackson, provided he kept his mind right. Well, of course he did get nearly that gigantic and he did not keep a cool head. But who could have? Even if his content was as uncontroversial as Justin Timberlake's, the fact of him being a really well prepared *white* rapper was gonna thrust him into uncharted realms of popularity. And nobody—I don't care who you are, even if you remain in Detroit and out of the limelight—can remain calm in the eye of that shitstorm.

Never mind those record sales from *The Slim Shady LP, The Marshall Mathers LP, The Eminem Show, 8 Mile,* and *Encore,* the awards he took home were enough to make a stoic cat lose himself. Right out of the gate he got rap Grammys for his first album and single. The next two albums won again, as did "Lose Yourself," from the *8 Mile* movie soundtrack. He won MTV awards, Best New Artist and overall Album of the Year Grammy nominations, American Music Awards, MTV Europe, Juno Awards, you name it. In "Lose Yourself" he even had the first rap track to win an Academy Award for Best Song. (Even though everybody halfway hip to hip hop is aware that Rakim's "Know the Ledge" from the Tupac flick *Juice* should have broken the rap line a decade earlier.)

Em isn't at all the type to desire this kind of mainstream acclaim, but he wasn't totally mad at it, either. He's a hardworking guy who can't help but want to better himself. What fucked with his brain was how politicians and pundits who didn't have shit to do with the music industry in particular or the entertainment industry in general were weighing in on him. You had *New York Times* political columnists pontificating on the meaning of him and his work. Lynn Cheney, that Dick V.P.'s wife, dissed him in front of the fuckin' United States Senate. (The bitch went: "So here's a name: Marshall Mathers. It is truly astonishing to me that a man whose work is so filled with hate would be so honored by his peers.") Now, yeah, Eminem sho' nuff liked to piss off stuffed shirts, but when you got him alone he'd admit that it was more than he bargained for. He would say that he asked for none of this. Dude just wanted to make a living off of rappin'.

And the effects of all the phony accolades and the boycotts and protests and drama with his trashy-ass mama showed. He might have withstood it all if he hadn't struggled with Kim. After their divorce, she gave birth to another nigga's kid, which fucked with him. But he was still in love with her! He'd fucked with Mariah Carey and a gang of fine and famous women. Yet Marshall and Kim went to the altar again in 2006. His best friend Proof, the model for Mekhi Phifer's character in *8 Mile*—was his best man. Less than eleven weeks later, man and wife were divorced.

Superstardom's a motherfucker. Ask Britney Spears. Or the guy Dre compared Marshall Mathers of Trailertown to initially, MJ. Or better yet, take a look at the life of Em. Since he'd broken through, he's been convicted of assault, been in and out of rehab, and even sparred with Moby. What really tore it for my man, though, was the shooting death of his best friend. Proof, aka DeShaun Holton, was the founder of the group D-12, and probably the second-biggest name in Detroit. He and Em loved each other in an open way, and Proof had a big cameo in *8 Mile*. He was the only rapper in the film to deliver a real freestyle for the cameras. On April 12, 2006, he was shot in the head by a bouncer at the CCC Club on 8 Mile Road after killing Keith Bender, a vet he was arguing with in the after-hours spot.

When I heard about his death, it was shocking for me to hear about the dude acting like that.

But a lot of people were like, "Ya know, Proof do talk a lot of shit."

Word is he was sayin' he was like "I'm the king of Detroit!" And shootin' niggas? I was like, "Proof?"

It's hard to say how a person is through and through. It was always about smiles and respect when I saw Proof. He was happy-go-lucky and uplifting. But our visits were always on some studio shit. Or we in the club. Or at a show or an awards event. It wasn't like, "Hey, let's go to the 'hoods of Detroit and just kick it."

My man shouldn't have been in an after-hours spot, not with his status and potential. But if a street cat of his fame *is* in a joint like that, it's gotta be on some low-key, keep-to-yourself vibe. If you *gotta* be in those places, make sure you do what you must and then come home safely. I wasn't there, so I can't say what exactly went wrong.

But I do know what the problem is with Proof's best friend. The death hit him devastatingly hard. In offering tribute at Proof's funeral—for which Dre uncharacteristically showed up—Marshall Mathers said: "He was a magnet. He lured you in. You wanted to learn about him, follow his swagger. Without Proof, there would be no Eminem, no Slim Shady, and no D-12." It was a testament also to the sincerity and tenderness of Eminem.

Nowadays it seems like the one-time poor kid's emotions are getting the better of him. He's isolated in Detroit, even from his own crew. For the longest time, one of the cats in D-12 had a sick child and no insurance and there's nothing he could do about it, in part because the man who makes the world even give a fuck about D-12 is cut off from the world. Now, Em's a grown man and all, but I put a lot of the responsibility for this phase of the dude's struggle on his management team. In the decade since he recorded *The Slim Shady LP*, Slim Shady hasn't done a whole lot, if you think about it. It's like, the first five years were action packed. Albums, movies, touring like a demon and helping develop 50 Cent. But recently? He mostly just hangs out like Bruce Wayne, a ghostly king of a genuflecting Detroit.

Paul Rosenberg and the people who run Shady Records have only focused on the one main guy, and when he's done there's no foundation for more. When Dre signed homeboy I thought it would be the making of a movement. I thought it would be Em who came up with new directions for Caucasian MCs like those found on Ego Trip's *The White Rapper Show* on VH1, not a bunch of *New York* magazine editors.

Mr. I Just Don't Give A Fuck I Got Brain Damage is acting again, and I truly hope it works out for him. It ought to work out; my man is talented as fuck. It's unlikely he'll ever recapture past MC glories, though. Think about it: What more can he really say? Even people who aren't even that into rap know more about this nigga than they do their next-door neighbor. We've heard it all already. Unless he actually gets up and does something that doesn't involve his daughter or cashing a paycheck.

Em is deep in the shit. And it didn't help that the guy he'd turned into almost as big a star as him, 50 Cent, was embroiled in epic beef with the guy *he* was supposed to be giving a leg up. These are the things that make artists quit rapping and move over to producing much sooner than their talents suggest they might.

The Game always had that rude-boy energy working for him. You know? That quality of chomping at the bit to diss. Anyone who's heard his work knows what I mean. I can remember listening to fresh vocals from him while hanging out in the studio with him, Busta Rhymes, and some of The Game's people. J-Boogie and Mike Lynn were around, too.

"You know what?" asked Busta Rhymes after taking in one particularly biting take, "When you're rappin', sometimes your shit is just so borderline *disrespectful*. I mean you really take it there!"

Everyone busted out laughing.

That's what's great about The Game. And that's his problem, too. His 2004 album, *The Documentary,* is the sound of someone struggling to keep up with the talent around him. He didn't always respect his place in the process. Making that album was a trip.

Jayceon Taylor was a kid from the streets of Compton who needed something else in his life to do, because the streets wasn't working for him. Dude was tight on the basketball court—he earned a scholarship to play at Washington State, then got kicked off campus behind some drug allegations—but the street shit kept that pro sports route from being an option. In almost no time he began to run with a hustler named D-Mack and got more known on the East Coast than out west. Dude had a lot of game, many different talents. He could rap, even if he wasn't a pure natural like, say, a Busta Rhymes.

Aftermath A&R man Mike Lynn went to bat for Taylor and got him signed to Aftermath. The kid had come to the label's attention after doing some one-off work with Bay Area indie kingpin JT Tha Bigga Figga. Doc felt really good to finally put a Compton kid into the game. And if The Game was about anything, both he and his mentor decided, it was going to be an extended salute to the idea of the hardcore West Coast MC. My boss knew exactly how powerful a force that rapper had been to music—shoot, to the culture—of humans on the planet. (These kids weren't just the bastards of Black Panther rebellion, they were a reaction to institutional Hollywood's program for Negroes to get over. It's like, I can feel Sydney Poitier and Will Smith as much as the next by-gosh-golly guy, but c'mon now: What were the studios ever gonna offer the average nigga?) Jayceon Taylor's whole musical persona was supposed to be the embodiment of that, from N.W.A. on up through to W.C. to that broke-ass kid on the Blue Line train who's hustlin' CDs and whose name you don't even know.

It took a while for The Game to develop as an MC. He spent over a year working more as a concept than as a bona fide rapper. During that time D-Mack wasn't doing too much for Game and he was on the hustle, grindin' on the streets doin' whatever was clever. It wouldn't have surprised me to learn that this nigga had been out sellin' MTA passes at Julian Dixon Station. I would run into him at various spots and he would complain about money and that no one was helping him. So I guess that's when he took the road like, I gotta look out for me. He was a cool guy; he just didn't have the right people around him.

It was Jimmy Iovine's idea to put The Game in G-Unit. At this point in Aftermath's development I was distant, but visible. And I was definitely watching how things took shape. There were compatibility problems between the Game and 50 from day one. Jimmy's idea was to have a West Coast presence in the crew to go with 50 and his New York sidekick Lloyd Banks and Young Buck, who was out of Nashville. 50 put them on, and these cats were G-Unit—Gorilla Unit—soldiers.

Big mistake. The Game was already on Aftermath. He was a work in progress and needed to be groomed, but he had his own dreams, like the Black Wall Street, his G-Unit equivalent business team. They were the ones who would oversee his sneaker deal and otherwise function as corporate thugs. The Game had his own people, Baron Davis of the Golden State Warriors and a bunch of other L.A. kids.

Unfortunately it took two years to make *The Documentary* because The Game couldn't write hooks. (It worked out cool, but dude is not as talented as his first album is good. Niggas don't understand that sometimes.) Reenter Curtis Jackson. Fiddy's a hook master, so their collaboration became a big part of the album.

But not as big as 50 said and not as little as The Game thinks. But Game's a kid, though; he should be allowed to make mistakes.

Anyway, they never got along, from day one. Dre loves that shit. The simple fact is that Dre actually likes an environment where everybody's got at least one gripe with *everyone* around the set. He feels that keeps everybody on their feet.

At first we kept things cool between The Game and 50 Cent by holding lots of meetings. We talked our way through the release of *The Documentary,* which would sell six million copies and become one of the biggest debuts in rap music history. Their differences really weren't that unusual; they just happened in public. And that made things go nuts. First there developed a war of words through radio airwaves and magazines. Next came the gunfire outside New York's Hot 97. After Fiddy and his people finished talking shit about The Game on air, the Compton kid's camp met them outside the station. One of the guns drawn by a G-Unit member went off, hit the sidewalk, then bounced up and struck The Game's cousin Peanut in the leg.

Then there was The Game's epic diss record "300 Bars" and his underground DVD accusing 50 of being a snitch. He went at Fiddy so hard, there was no way they could remain labelmates. Dre and Jimmy ended up taking Jayceon off of Aftermath and moving him over to its sister label, Geffen. The whole episode turned into one of the biggest rap stories of the millennium. But 50 Cent and The Game at least managed to come out alive. So far.

By the time his showdown with Kanye West came around, Fiddy had it down to a science. You could all but hear the circus music in their "showdown" in September 2007.

Chapter Sixteen

Detox

I wasn't around so much for the recording of The Game's debut, especially at the end. If anybody knew how burned out I'd gotten on Interscope/Aftermath bullshit, it was my wife. She brought up the idea of revisiting nightclub management.

"Viv, the club was cool and everything, but I'm just not into doing anything at somebody else's spot. If we can't own it and run it ourselves, if we can't really make money off of it, then I don't want to do it. I'm tired of making money for everybody else."

Vivian kept on me, though, and we discussed a concept. She sat me down and we started writing a business proposal for an upscale sports bar and hired a professional to shape up the document. Then it was time to look for investors. That one was tough. The one thing I never had experience with was securing investors. Interscope was that super-milky teat, and I didn't know much about other financial nourishment.

"I'll go find some investors," Vivian said, with a confidence that didn't make total sense to me.

"And I'll just keep doin' what I'm doin'," I said.

What I'd be doin' was sitting front row at that pointless altercation between Fiddy and The Game.

While all of this third-generation beef nonsense was taking shape, Jimmy began asking for *Detox*. *Detox* is the concept Dre had been trying to fully conceptualize for years. He was so serious at one point just after the second *Chronic* album that he had T-shirts made up. These featured the word "Detox" with that universal red, crossed-line prohibition circle around it. It was the farewell album he would walk off to, the one that might show him graduating from gangsta rap, basically. It made sense, going from *The Chronic* to *Detox,* because that's what Dre had done, basically. The problem was, he didn't know what to write about. Who wanted to hear about his stable, suburban life? And how in good conscience could he be shouting "Fuck tha Police!" or some such shit at this point in his life?

Dre's an elusive joker. But even he wasn't sure he could pull off the album that was supposed to be his final artistic representation.

When The Game said on his second album, *Doctor's Advocate,* that he's been watchin' Dre so long he's making beats now, it didn't really mean much. It's his blessing and his curse, his inclination to talk hella shit. It's typical. Here's another prime example:

The spring of its release, we were at Encore studio: We were in the front room with DJ Hi-Tek, just kickin' it. Snoop was there, as well as The Game's people. And The Game started a little shit-talkin' about Bow Wow, knowing full well that the kid is a nephew of Snoop's, just like him.

"Yo dog," Snoop said, right in the middle of The Game goin' off. "You my nigga. Li'l Bow Wow's my nigga," Snoop told him. "You know what, since he's my li'l nigga too, we don't need to be talkin' about dude like that. We don't even need to be discussin' that shit."

For an O.G. like Snoop to say that shit in front of everybody, that's what I call guidance. He was lettin' him know: It's bigger than what you think. It's all about beefin' to these cats. They think they have to have beef in their lives to sell a record. Dude's chased beef with 50, with niggas from the Roc-a-Fella camp, with Ras Kass, Yukmouth, with Death Row, Joe Budden, I could go on and on. Young cats like Game need to have the confidence in themselves just to be out there rockin' *without* the beef and just do what they do. *Then* the sky's the limit. Until then, ain't none of these rappers really gonna kick a hole in the sky and take things to the next level.

Look, I like Game. Jayceon's an outstanding individual. He just really needs a lot more guidance. He's a hustler—will hustle his ass off. But if you think about it though, he sat on the label for *two years,* went out there hustlin' mixtapes and makin' money. Then he went through periods when he thought that Aftermath and Interscope didn't give a fuck. He just needed to get his talent a little more focused and he didn't want to wait.

Mike Lynn and Dre decided to stick with him. Then when he was put in G-Unit, complicated as things were, it all started happening for him. 50 gave him great songs that he had been saving for his own album. Both of *The Documentary*'s great hit songs—"Hate It or Love It" and "How We Do" were 50's songs. So, he should have been appreciative, no matter how fucked up parts of the situations were. And if he wasn't appreciative, how do you think 50 felt?

Like I said, The Game is a good dude, with lots of personality and hustle. He's just hella extra when it comes to doin' dumb shit. Jayceon's got to change his lifestyle. You'll know he's done that when he stops talking about Dre in his rhymes. It's Jayceon's training wheels, the ones his old ass won't take off. Once he moves on to another subject the world will know that he's ready to stand on his own. If he'd had guidance and watched his p's and q's he'd be bigger than 50 right now. His second album was good. He had his songs played everywhere. But just imagine how big he'd be if he still had Dre and 50.

By this time I was pulling away, trying to get my projects going. Dre seemed happier to do stuff with outside people, as he did with his old friend DJ Pooh on *The Wash.* That one at least made sense to me because Pooh used to drive Dre to work back before he hit it big. And he's the talented one who wrote *Friday* with Ice Cube. But Pooh hadn't the day-to-day long-term experience that Dre and I shared, so the two of them getting a project done felt like a snub.

But Pooh is an undeniable talent. It was much harder watching the kinds of clowns he brought in. Like that nigga Lonnie, who Dre thought was only about dollars, not great music. I never understood why Dr. Dre kept cats around him who he said were not good dudes or who were untalented. But every other word out their mouths would be "Dre."

I started focusing more on my sons, Sir and Mister. When they got old enough, I put a lot into their sports, all but living through them. Sir, in particular, I fell into grooming. Between that and school, it took all my time. My sons—both sensitive Sir and laid-back Mister—showed me there's a whole lot more to life than the music industry. In time, Prince Bo Williams would arrive and give me even more to live for.

Above all else I'm glad there's a woman who isn't always feeling the music.

"But Dad lets us listen to it!"

My baby Vivian, still shapely after delivering three children, believes in preserving innocence. If only she could go back and find mine.

"I don't care what your dad lets you listen to," my boys' mother tells them. "I'm not your dad."

Pop and alternative rock stay on when she drives. I'm not that tight on those genres of music, so I appreciate what she brings to the table. Not only does my wife limit my own gangsta baggage, she broadens the horizons of these boys I love so much.

Lots of dudes need a girl like Vivian.

Dre had help procrastinating in developing the farewell album *Detox*. Help ain't really the right word. It's more like excuses. It's hard enough tryina jump into a project you feel conflicted about. He wasn't a gangsta and, as a producer, that was fine. His only job was bringing his artists' music to life. The new songs Dr. Dre did with 50 Cent and The Game were the pinnacle of what gangsta rap can be. Sometime, just as a barometer, listen to "In Da Club" and "Boyz-N-The-Hood" back to back and in that order. It's like watching *The*

Great Train Robbery right after you see *The Departed*; it's hard to fathom how far the form has come.

Years were passing in the wake of the first conceptualization of the *Detox* album. First word of it came when we were first working with The Game. But, as I said, Dre had excuses, some of them from the very place where the demands came from. When Dre would really get on a roll with an idea, he'd want to seclude himself in Hawaii and in studio and do his damn thing. And it seemed the few times dude actually had a lead on what the album could be like, Jimmy would be on the phone. "Get back to L.A. and work with Gwen Stefani." Or, "I need you to do a remix from the Interscope album that ain't really selling."

He got paid, alright, for this extra shit—as he did when he produced outside cats like Jay-Z—but it kept him away from *Detox,* which deep down is what he knew he ought to be doing.

When that beef between 50 Cent and The Game went public, Al Sharpton called over and asked for half a million dollars. Otherwise he was going to bring the heat on behalf of "The Community." We gave him $250,000. Then we had The Game and 50 make up in public, holding an elaborate press conference. If you ever watch the footage, you can tell neither one of our artists was into it. They gave money to charities in New York and in Compton, but their beef just got worse and worse. Part of the reason is that their making up was strictly a show. This is the sort of thing that we, as hip-hop artists and entrepreneurs, have to put up with.

Regardless of who was right and wrong in this complicated beef, they were both talented cats—legitimate artists. They sold a bunch of albums because their raw skills were developed to one extent or another.

That's an exception in today's music industry. Even going back to the biz past and the early '90s heyday of Death Row, hip hop has lacked a system for developing artists. Take Berry Gordy and what he did at Motown. Yeah, all them cats and all them chicks he recorded were from the streets. But he taught them eitiquette. He taught them how to *talk* to motherfuckers. He took them to kick it with kings and queens, and they knew what to say and how to act. Yeah, they were the same niggas that hung out in the 'hood, but they learned to adjust.

If Prince came out today, with high heels and the purple shit, would he sell? Would the world accept him? When he came out in the late 1970s, the system allowed him to be creative. Not like the system of today. The Britney Spears era (and the technology issues) of the first part of the century have made people in the business totally forget about the true artist in favor of the manufactured artist.

Just based on the way things are run, you would think that the fake musician makes more money than the true artist. But that's not the way it turns out to be. I've learned that, CD for CD, the true artist makes more than the manufactured artist. These people aren't in for two or three hit songs. They don't disappear after a couple of albums.

People forget that it took Prince three full albums to catch on. He wouldn't have even made it to the part where he could produce a *1999*. Look at D'Angelo.

Or take Gnarls Barkley. Atlantic Records fought Cee-Lo tooth and nail. They told him it wasn't gonna work. But he and bandmate Brian Burton believed in it, and it's one of the few albums that went platinum in an anemic 2006.

The problem with the business is the top-heaviness of the executives. Aside from there being too many execs, the ones who are there can't relate to genuinely creative personalities. They don't give a fuck about the creative artist. That's why popular music is the way it is today.

When I say that hip hop exacts a cost, I'm talking about a lot more than business. Maybe the ultimate example is what went down with Dre and his ol' lady—my old friend the singer Michel'le.

As I said before, I was extremely tight with Michel'le, back in my early L.A. days. We were tight—if not quite like brother and sister, then something close to that. We talked all the time. I knew she wasn't particularly fond of Suge, but she really did like Dre. They always would argue, though, so it never worked between them. Plus, they had Marcel, Dre's son who is the spitting image of his dad. So that relationship was always tense.

When Dre and I decided to leave Death Row, me and Michel'le were—to say the least—not on the same page, just because I was cool with Dre, the ex she never really got over. But sometimes you learn about people in their absence. It was easy for me to think I knew Dre's homegirl during the relative good times, when Michel'le was working and being famous and life was a swirling upward breeze.

Next though, Michel'le surprised the shit out of me and got with Suge. I guess maybe Suge is some kind of charming motherfucker and his millions weren't exactly a turn-off, but goddamn. There's hella niggas in L.A. who ain't named Suge. Why couldn't she get with them?

Who knows, maybe it was a simple case of love, but the very idea seems like some bullshit, no doubt. It's a lot more believable that Michel'le just hated Dre that badly, resented him that much. A resentment born out of spurned love.

But like I said, everybody in hip hop gets fucked. Dre got screwed doubly when you consider that Michel'le being with Suge meant that his sworn enemy was raising Marcel, who was becoming a young man. She knew about every fucked-up thing that Suge has done and yet she would expose her son to that? Wow. Love *really* will make people do crazy things.

Marcel and I used to go to the same barber, Eclipse Salon, out in the Valley. We'd talk while we waited for a chair to open up, choppin' up about almost anything. Marcel, when he was just a little one, was a presence in the studio. He sat right next to the board with me and Dre. Shit, I can tell you what Marcel likes on his burgers, the first girl he kissed. We talked about everything while waiting for those haircuts. So, it was no problem asking about his real father.

"Marcel, would you like to see your father?"

"Yeah, man," Marcel answered without a second's fraction of pause. "I want to see my dad."

"Let me hook something up," I told the boy.

I knew Michel'le's mother, still had her number and address. It wouldn't be too hard to work something out.

How fucked up did Dre feel about this intractable blemish on his fatherhood record? How neutralized? How conflicted that he could move masses across the globe, yet not be able to keep his seed from being watered with the Blood-born hostility of Marion "Suge" Knight? It's a crushing realization that my man lived with every day. Now, just think about that for a moment: This nigga you just split ties with? Raising your son? It's fucked up.

I felt fucked up. So you know Dre felt fucked up.

Andre Young did a lot of great stuff with and for his children over the years, including taking care of Nicole's kids fathered by her ex-husband, former Laker guard Sedale Threatt. It was lot more than Threatt's punk ass would do. Once, I took their boy Tyler to visit his father, whom Sedale hadn't seen in more than a year. In a half hour he was calling me back, already done with seeing the boy.

As a father of three who doesn't miss a Little League game if at all possible, I think you've got to be a sick, sorry-ass motherfucker if that's the most you want to see your child under such circumstances. Fuck Sedale Threatt. I commend Nicole for getting Tyler away from that dude and Dre for all he's done in raising that boy in addition to his own blood offspring.

Still, the Aftermath crew found the domestic situation with Marcel disheartening. It wasn't even something you could talk about. It's like, my man's got a gang of kids—thirteen, according to some reports; we've never even gone there—but this still had to hurt. Dre didn't talk about it a lot to us, the supposed members of his inner circle.

Dre's a sensitive artist and shit. It's not like he's not a tough guy, though. To be great takes that mixture and Dre embodies that. It's like the saying goes, creativity at its highest level is extreme discipline and extreme un-discipline, side by side. An artist has to be able to wild out *and* hold back. Dre can be hard. Once, when he was eleven, he kept to himself for months that he had a broken collarbone.

That nigga held a lot of that shit in. But, if you think about the situation with Michel'le's boy, what could he possibly say? I mean, *really*. That Marcel situation is some crazy-ass shit. Imagine what it did to his work relationships, in terms of his crew's regard for him. C'mon, we obviously loved the guy, but this happening to the *leader* of us? Where are we headed as a crew? We're supposed to be running through a wall for this man and, oh by the way, Jimmy's on the other line demanding a jerk of your very short leash. In a subtle way, it bred insecurity and deflated us.

By 2006, there was still no *Detox* album. And Jimmy really wanted it. Or, to be precise, all of their bosses at Seagram's wanted it. Even if it was only Jimmy, the pressure alone would have been enough to get most artists' asses in gear. Dre knew exactly how tough the head man at Interscope is. That dude is ruthless.

Once, way back in the Death Row days, I was in a meeting with Dre that took place in Jimmy's office. Jimmy's secretary interrupted.

"Gerardo is on line two!"

"I don't wanna talk to that guy," Jimmy told the secretary. I was shocked. Gerardo, with his "Rico Suave" song, made stupid money for Jimmy, back when Interscope was on shaky ground. That should have been my first lesson that it was never about personal relationships around there. Just business.

My second lesson was what went down next. Jimmy fielded a series of phone calls with abrupt put-downs. In a nutshell, each query got answered with the equivalent of a gruff, "Hell, naw!"

I asked Jimmy what he would do if one of the Interscope staff had talked to him like that.

"I'd give him a raise," Jimmy said.

"Give him a raise?" I asked out of confusion.

"Yes, a big raise and then I'd encourage him to buy a big house. Then after he was fully committed financially, I'd demote him."

I was starting to get the picture.

"Because after that," Jimmy continued, "his family life would be fucked up. His pussy would be ruined. Everything. Yep, I'd give him a raise."

Anyway, this time, finally, *Detox* had to happen. Or so everyone was saying. But what I knew is that nobody from the old crew wanted to fuck with Dre. Mike Elizondo didn't want to surround himself with what he saw as the untalented yes-men who dominated Dre's camp. Kon Artist, the D-12 member and superproducer in his own right, wasn't ready to fuck with Dre, either. Even Mel-Man, who had fallen out with his one-time piano crony over some things Mel-Man had said in an interview, was shying away from Dr. Dre.

Then what had to happen, happened: Jimmy demanded that Dre go out and reassemble his old crew. It was like Blues Brothers on the gangsta tip, but only if you think of Jimmy Iovine as an old nun and imagine Aftermath/Interscope/Seagram's as a very corrupt church.

Dre's effort to make an old-school artsy hip-hop record in the mode of De La Soul failed when Busta Rhymes's *The Big Bang Theory* didn't sell.

I feel bad for Busta. He's had a lot of negativity in his aura and can't help but wonder what he's done to bring that shit to him. When his bodyguard got shot and he kept quiet, you knew the bad feeling would be surrounding him for a while. Let's be real: Busta knows the rap thing is over. Maybe he should have focused more on acting. He never struck me as comfortable focusing on being hard and competing with young people on the grounds of a twenty-first-century MC. People forget that the first Leaders of the New School album was recorded right after the first George Bush was inaugurated!

Hip hop will always be a young man's game. Dre was struggling to get just his third solo album together, so you didn't have to sell that nigga on this point.

It's more than a matter of age, though. Between what's gone on with Trevor—as Busta's mother calls him—and Marshall and Jayceon and Curtis, you can't help but see what's wrong with the Aftermath structure. Sure, a lot of it's about Mr. Fuck tha Police feeling a hip-hop artist has to find his own path—and their built-in edginess is what brought them to his attention anyway. But at Aftermath there's almost no investment in artist development. You've got to prepare talent for what it's like to sell five million albums in a relentlessly media-driven environment. Based on the numbers we've seen over the past years, will we ever see an artist sell six million CDs again? Six million units of an Internet something or other, maybe. Six million ringtones, maybe. But that era of people buying shiny little discs that they listen to in their cars? That shit ain't happening no more. And these crazy ghetto motherfuckers carried the ball the very last drive up the marketplace.

The Big Bang is an incredible album, one of the most artistic of 2006. "The Ghetto," which is based on a Rick James sample, is one of the best, most musically ambitious songs I've heard in a decade; the record just didn't do the numbers that it should have. And falling short is commonplace in today's music business. And just like everybody else, almost ain't nearly good enough when you got that famous name that rhymes with Dr. J.

"So, Dre, where's that album?" Jimmy would ask.

Chapter Seventeen

The Rebirth of West Coast Hip Hop

D re and I had grown distant and the rapport had gotten so bad between us that I was reduced to running errands for his wife. And know that Nicole is controlling. She's the type who fires maids almost frivolously. There have been so many housekeepers taking the train back from the Valley, pink slips in hand, that a casual observer like me can't keep count. And here I was running errands for her snotty ass.

Nicole couldn't really boss me around like the average maid because I was so close to her husband. But, still, she did. Somehow it reminded me that I'd always had all the keys to everything, from studios to that old Death Row penthouse apartment on Wilshire Boulevard. Really, this was as far as I'd come. Here I was in a power struggle with a diva housewife—and I wasn't even interested in power; she was. It was depressing. Watching her hold back from going off on me like she went off on other people, I thought about the projects that never came to pass. And it felt a little like too much of my life had been surrendered.

So, Nicole and I weren't getting along, for a long time. She couldn't go off on me; she knew where the roots of our relationships with Andre Young lay. And while that did bring about elements of mutual respect, it also ratcheted up the tension between us. She couldn't help but feel threatened by my spiritual and historical proximity to her husband, while I felt diminished by the kind of work I'd been reduced to. And her sense that I was ungrateful to be in her service made me less assertive than I might normally be.

My difficult relationship with Dre's wife incensed me—maybe even depressed me—but I took it. Same as I took so many of her husband's promises. Nobody in the crew could make anything happen anywhere in the industry, despite the loyalty we'd shown him. Jimmy? That cat Dre would run through a wall for, because Jimmy enabled him. It was obvious now that all of his promises of—and even preliminary development of—TV and film and record projects were just efforts to appease us. But we were gonna stick this thing out because I know the potential of his clout. And I'm tryin' not to trip too hard because I'm still doing my thing. I'm still meeting people. Magic still returns my calls, promptly.

Yet it did suck that no one on the team could get a noteworthy project together. People at Bad Boy were able to do their thing. So were kids at Roc-a-Fella, So So Def and other notable labels. And it's not that everybody couldn't agree on a project. It's that everybody agreed on it and then we go to work and Dre was like, "Hold up: I went over and talked to Jimmy . . ." And our take was, "I don't know what Jimmy done told ya, but now you're tellin' us to hold up." How many times does that have to happen?

Thing is, Dre had begun to fancy himself a businessman. I could see through all of that. Dre didn't start making money, liquid money to where he had cash in the bank, until Aftermath. So, I was the one who would talk to the accountant. Millions and millions slipped through Andre Young's hands. Before Aftermath, he didn't sign shit. He didn't write checks, he didn't sign nothin'. I had to go get everything. He wouldn't do no paperwork. It was even to the point where if he wanted to work with somebody you had to get him on the line and talk to him first.

Where did this urge come from? He never told me. It could be that Dre was simply emulating Jimmy. Just as likely, the impetus could have come from watching his peers—the Puffys, the Jay-Zs—grow in stature and cross over from hip hop. I was never convinced that business is where his head belonged. His background wasn't that of a successful drug dealer. He wasn't someone who put money over music, like that middling Bad Boy producer. And this nonsense with me and Nicole felt like just another example of my friend not handling his business. Where, really, would Andre Young have been without Bruce Williams?

About all Dre had learned about business was to try to do to his people what they saw Jimmy do to him. And we just couldn't believe it. We was *with* Dre when the suits at Interscope tried to do the same stuff to him. And now he was trying to do it to us. My friend was acting as if we did not know.

Through all the turmoil, the artists themselves sometimes change. And when they change is that good for hip hop and the people in hip hop? Or is it just trying to be a businessman when you aren't really a businessman.

Here's an example: We were on tour. Our crew is four or five guys. Snoop's got twenty-five to thirty people in his entourage. Cube got a sizable contingent. And Dr. Dre is the one who's headlining the tour! The way things were structured, we had problems getting requests as simple as a motherfuckin' backstage pass. How ill is that? Why we got problems and nobody else got problems? This is *our* tour. It was senseless and, frankly, demeaning.

Of course our crew complained to me about it. And I'm like, *dude, they give me the same shit*. I had to ask, "Dre, are you sticking up for niggas? Why we getting this kinda shit?" On the *2001* tour these muthafuckas should have been listening to what we had to say. They shouldn't have been outnumbering us.

It's not a personal matter. Backstage passes didn't mean shit to me, because everybody knows what I do, and I can get what I need to get anyway. But the point is why did the Aftermath staff have to constantly get shitted on by management when Snoop and them got to do what-

ever they wanted. The bottom line is Dre would talk tough but do little or nothing. He didn't stick up for us. At the time, Snoop was everywhere, doing appearances on TV and DVDs—everywhere. And *he* was
putting his boys in the game. They were all doing their thing. It was
difficult to watch. Dr. Dre's crew could get nothing going. We might
as well have been toiling on behalf of some unremarkable journey-
man entertainer.

So, if a boss doesn't stick up for his people and years and years and
years go by, shit gets deeper. Niggas get older. Eventually, the crew
gets to be like, *Yo. Time out.*

Let's say you got a friend who's fucked up sometimes in the things
that he do. You still stick it out with him. There comes a point,
though, where a nigga like me can't take any more. I had to approach
Dre about it. So we sat down to have this talk. I was blunt.

"Yo, dog, why I gotta do all this stuff?"

The guy I thought of as my best friend on the planet was evasive
about my future with him.

"Man," Dre starts up, "you gotta figure out exactly what it is you
want to do."

An awkward silence followed.

"Yeah? I been trying to figure that out for a long time."

Then we talked about the Nicole stuff. And it wasn't drama. I know
he's got his own drama with Jimmy and Nicole and all of his yes-men
and temperamental young bucks like Fiddy and The Game to deal
with. I got that. After all we had been through, a conversation like this
could never be tense. And I felt like he knew what I was talking about
the very moment I said it.

Dre made a surprising admission, before I really got started complaining. Maybe that's because Dre knows how I am once I really get
started complaining.

"I know you felt like you were being belittled."

"Yeah, I did. I never could understand why I had to do those kinds of things, with all the work I put in and all the stuff that I've been promised."

"Man," he said, like it hurt him to speak, "I don't think you really appreciate nothin'."

That was crazy to me. It sounded rehearsed. I knew this was Nicole talking. Same as when he told people over and over that it was his wife who got him to give up that post–Death Row "positive" Dre image. Shit, we *all* told him to drop that nonstarter of an idea.

Anyway, Dre went on.

"You don't send nobody no thank you cards or nothin'."

That was bananas to me. Only when other people said it did I even acknowledge that his career would have definitely been smaller, to any degree imaginable, if I hadn't been there for him, shielding him from all the bullshit so that he could focus on music. I'd hardly let myself *think* that thought over the past fourteen years. Now hearing this, I felt that thought. A part of me wanted to be like, *Nigga, shut the fuck up.*

Instead, I was like, "Dog: I've told you thanks on a continuous thank you."

And that's honestly all I remember about that conversation.

Chapter Eighteen

Givin' Props

I thought long and hard about what Dre said that night, even if the words coming out of his mouth seemed largely scripted by his wife. And I can't front; a lot of what you've read in this book so far, the ups and downs, are a way of showing how much I appreciate Dre and the things he's done for me.

I've not just ridden with Dre. I've ridden *for* Dre. I've done the jobs that he won't and can't do.

I ran into Warren G. And as hot as we were to talk about his future music projects, we couldn't do that without talking about the heyday of his "G-Funk Era." And that meant we had to deal with the fact that Andre Young, Warren's own brother, didn't sign him.

"Why did you have to go to Def Jam, in New York, when you were right here? You brought 213 to Death Row. Shit, you introduced Snoop to Dre."

Of all of Dre's dodgy decisions through the years, this one, which happened before I was even on the scene, had nagged at me as much as any.

"I could never understand why Dre didn't put his foot down. He never said, 'Put Warren in the lineup,' " I said.

"But Bruce," he answered, looking old and wise a lot earlier than I once would have expected, "what if he *had* put his foot down?"

Goddamn, what a question. In truth, big brother not demanding his way was better for his Warren. Gentle Warren on Death Row just wouldn't have worked out; he and Warren and Suge didn't really get along. All through the Death Row years Suge and Snoop had been able to put their Blood and Crip differences aside. But Warren was the one exception. Suge treated him badly. Anyway, Warren went and sold a bunch of records under Russell Simmons's organization. More important, he managed to do so without getting shot or permanently scarred.

In hindsight it was now possible to see that my friend and colleague did a little something like that for me, too. He had made it so that Jimmy couldn't control me. Suge couldn't control me. It's undeniable that I got stuck in the middle of things, but Dre kept me away from the truly hard core bullshit. Despite all the opportunities I thought I'd missed, here I was now a record exec with green-light clearance. And the stuff I'd learned about what makes for great records, as well of the pitfalls of inadequate artist development, could not have been more tangible in any situation imaginable.

I'm still kind of a young cat, and yet I've got a great story. My youth gig spanned the era of the first *Friday* and a skinny nigga with a fade crooning "I-8-7 on an undercover cop" to that hot song about rims that your little sister downloaded yesterday. I was dead-up in the mix when thug violence went from backstreet reality to front-page news and hip hop crossed over from funkiest nightclubs to the cover of *Forbes* magazine. It was also a beautiful, contradictory time, a place on God's timeline that will always have a gold star by it because it's when street niggas got paid. And my time will always have an asterisk by it, because gangsta rap always breaks the rules.

I think back to one of the last really great times I had in connection with the biz. There was no Dre, no Suge, no Jimmy Iovine. It was me and Mel-Man, back when the second *Chronic* album was still selling. He knew an activist from the 'hood who could get us entrance to the World Conference on Racism in Dearborn, South Africa. Protestors who were angry at the United States for not sending Colin Powell as a delegate carried posters depicting the highest-ranking American black man as a lapdog to the president.

We stayed at President François Botha's house. It turned out that we were the first black people ever to stay there, which was huge. Botha's place is the equivalent to Camp David, with armed guards, golf courses, and a self-contained railroad track, all right on the ocean.

The trip allowed me, for the very first time, to consider what young people on the international scene were into, what the average girl on a township street might be thinking. Kids everywhere knew Tupac, just like they knew Biggie. In the townships, we learned of gangs called the Tupac Boys and the Dre Boys. It told me that the music is so powerful that a concept can travel the world.

We learned about how little of the money from AIDS charities and benefits actually makes it to the people it's intended to help. It was ridiculous, the way middlemen opened stores and bought homes instead of aiding children and families that have been ripped apart by the disease. As a delegate to the conference, I was privy to information that's not shared so much stateside. It was a lot of information. In one session, 300 young people locked arm in arm walked in and vented about their faces being plastered on posters around the country. They were mad that they hadn't gotten a dime of financial support in return.

I felt so fucked up. It was like we had visited a tinderbox. Something seemed bound to go down.

We walked on a part of the beach that had no sand. It was all rocks. Here, the railroad tracks came to a stop. Walking, Mel-Man and I saw a pool that was cut into the rocks. A dark, gloomy feeling came across us as we approached it. We noticed a series of brick houses surrounding the pool. The rocks around it were razor sharp. It turns out that this pool existed for the pure purpose of washing recalcitrant slaves out to sea.

So much of this education was painful for me.

The famous terror attacks of 2001 happened a week after we returned from the conference. It was super-weird to have all that drama go on so soon after our return. I knew I was seeing the recent events differently from most after our experience in South Africa. Hip hop sure enough had to take me far from home to show me what life was all about. So far, that trip represents the pinnacle of my post–Shit Tier education.

Ted Howard was a partner of mine from D.C. He was a producer who, like so many others, had been trying to get his music heard by Dre. What I brought to Dre was pretty good, but the two never hooked up. Ted and I stayed in touch, grabbing a drink together if he was in my town, or more likely, I was in his.

We were shooting the shit, catching up on things, when I told him that I had a business plan for a sports bar. All I needed was the dough.

"Sheeitt," Ted murmured over his beverage. "I can get a $2.5 million line of credit. Let me in on that sports bar!"

Ted's contribution helped Vivian to secure a commercial agent who set up a meeting with an investment group that owned a lot of downtown L.A. Over the course of eighteen months the investment group entertained our idea. They liked our plans and wanted to be our partner. But before they would put up the seven-figure amount needed to lease the site Viv and I had chosen—the historic Pacific Gas building on Flower Street that was adjacent to the Staples Center—they had to hear the detailed plan in person.

I stood before an entire group of high-profile businessmen and gave them our vision of the sports bar/club from private luxury boxes to a European-style of serving cuisine to the holograms of great L.A. sports figures.

My presentation had felt natural and easy. I could only think back to my career in music. My ability to pull off what I just did could only have come from watching Jimmy and Suge. But, also, to a lesser degree, I needed to give props to Tupac, 50 Cent and The Game. Maybe even Robin and how she ran her girls around. My hip-hop family made the game look easy.

Afterward my investors, Sean and Freddie, took me aside. They not only thought that I'd knocked the pitch out of the park, they also wanted me to join them on another business they had brewing.

In hindsight, things have gone down between me and the biz exactly as they are supposed to.

Experience was the salary at both Death Row and Aftermath. My genius friend can be irresponsible and self-absorbed, but the cat can teach a lesson in his own special way.

I'm happy where I am now. I helped make history with my man Dre. And I got to witness the strengths of street knowledge—and its weaknesses. And even if a part of me wishes I could have been there to watch the Doctor struggle through another album-patient, I'm not complaining in the least. It ain't all bad being the man next to da man.

Ta-Dow!

Acknowledgments

Bruce Williams:

Thanks:

To God, my wife and sons. Melody Guy and Frank Scatoni. My mother, Esther L. Roberts. Andre Young for the travels in the hip-hop world. Magic Johnson for helping me believe in myself. Donnell Alexander for his hard work in making me look good. Foressiah, thanks for taking care of the boys. Thanks to everyone that has love for me and the ones that don't, I got love for you. To my investors of my sports bar in downtown L.A., thanks for believing in me. To my brothers Jamus and Matthew, and my sister Cherelle. I'd also like to thank hip hop. Braxton: it was your idea to write this book, which ended up helping me in ways that I couldn't imagine. Deepest thanks also to the Tyler family, Chestis, and Kenya June June.

Donnell Alexander

Thanks:

Perry Crowe, Melody Guy, Greg Dinkin, Frank Scatoni, Mindy Farabee, Ronin Ro, Arthur Africano, Laini Coffee, Brendan Mullen, Lloyd Francis, Gary Kazanjian, and Lisa K. Ferguson, all of my kids and their moms, and Vivian and Bruce for showing me a different world and introducing me to their children. And of course, Neille Ilel, who kept me above water during high tide.

About the Authors

BRUCE WILLIAMS was Dr. Dre's go-to-guy for almost two decades, having been involved in every aspect of Dre's personal and professional life. An actor, screenwriter, and film/TV producer, Williams, now owner of a sports bar in downtown Los Angeles, is currently working on a cable-TV pilot based on his experiences as "the man next to the man."

DONNELL ALEXANDER has written about hip hop and African culture in America for the *Los Angeles Times, Utne Reader,* and *The Source,* and was a senior staff editor for *Los Angeles CityBeat.* His essay "Cool Like Me: Are Black People Cooler than White People?" is a staple of university curricula and has been widely anthologized. He also writes literary criticism for the *San Francisco Chronicle,* and is the author of the forthcoming novel *Rhyme Scheme.*

About the Type

This book was set in Garamond, a typeface originally designed by the Parisian typecutter Claude Garamond (1480–1561). This version of Garamond was modeled on a 1592 specimen sheet from the Egenolff-Berner foundry, which was produced from types assumed to have been brought to Frankfurt by the punchcutter Jacques Sabon.

Claude Garamond's distinguished romans and italics first appeared in *Opera Ciceronis* in 1543–44. The Garamond types are clear, open, and elegant.